CHINA IN THE 21ST CENTURY

WHAT EVERYONE NEEDS TO KNOW®

CHINA IN THE 21ST CENTURY

WHAT EVERYONE NEEDS TO KNOW®

3rd Edition

JEFFREY N. WASSERSTROM AND MAURA ELIZABETH CUNNINGHAM

OXFORD
UNIVERSITY PRESS

OXFORD
UNIVERSITY PRESS

Oxford University Press is a department of the University of Oxford. It furthers
the University's objective of excellence in research, scholarship, and education
by publishing worldwide. Oxford is a registered trade mark of Oxford University
Press in the UK and certain other countries.

"What Everyone Needs to Know" is a registered trademark
of Oxford University Press.

Published in the United States of America by Oxford University Press
198 Madison Avenue, New York, NY 10016, United States of America.

Library of Congress Cataloging-in-Publication Data
Names: Wasserstrom, Jeffrey N., author. | Cunningham, Maura Elizabeth, author.
Title: China in the 21st century : what everyone needs to know /
Jeffrey N. Wasserstrom and Maura Elizabeth Cunningham.
Other titles: China in the twenty-first century Description: 3rd edition. |
Oxford ; New York : Oxford University Press, 2018. |
Series: What everyone needs to know
Identifiers: LCCN 2017058669 | ISBN 9780190659080 (pbk. : alk. paper) |
ISBN 9780190659073 (hardback : alk. paper)
Subjects: LCSH: China—History—21st century.
Classification: LCC DS779.4 .W376 2018 | DDC 951.06—dc23
LC record available at https://lccn.loc.gov/2017058669

3 5 7 9 8 6 4

Paperback printed by Webcom Inc., Canada
Hardback printed by Bridgeport National Bindery, Inc., United States of America

CONTENTS

Part II   The Present and the Future

4 From Mao to Now   **75**

5 US–China Misunderstandings   119

PREFACE TO THE THIRD EDITION

In October 2012, as we finished work on the second edition of this book, we worried about superseding events that might occur between the time we signed off on the proofs and the time the first copies hit bookshelves. Our concern focused, naturally enough, on the book's final questions and answers, in the chapter titled "The Future" that closes the volume. As historians, we are always leery about veering, even cautiously, into the realm of prediction, but we had a more specific reason to feel uneasy: a once-in-a-decade leadership transition was about to take place in Beijing. In November 2012, Hu Jintao was scheduled to relinquish his hold on a post he had occupied since November 2002, that of general secretary of the Chinese Communist Party (CCP). He was expected to follow that up early in 2013 by stepping down from being president of the People's Republic of China (PRC) and being replaced as chairman of the Central Military Commission. We were fairly confident that Hu would not try to retain any of those positions. We also felt pretty certain that Xi Jinping, long Hu's designated heir-apparent, would take on all three of the vacated posts. Surprising things, however, had been happening in Chinese elite politics during the preceding two years. Most notably, the charismatic Bo Xilai had gained popularity. His rise was curtailed by a sensational scandal early in 2012 (discussion about which we had included in the book, of course), but it had seemed that Bo might prove a wild card, capable of derailing the long-anticipated smooth passing of the baton from Hu to Xi. Even after Bo's downfall, questions and rumors swirled around the leadership transition, and we hesitated to say definitively that Xi would become China's next paramount leader.

Determined to avoid having anything we wrote about the transition proven wrong before the book even shipped, we sought and received permission from Oxford University Press to delay signing off on the second edition's language until Xi's ascent was assured. We were ready to do this as soon as Xi was installed as leader of the CCP and the other members of the new Politburo Standing Committee he would head were announced in November 2012. After he stepped into that role, we felt comfortable saying that the Hu era had ended and the Xi era had begun. We were confident that he would assume the other two positions in due course, and sure enough he did in March 2013, while the second edition was in production. (What we did not foresee—but no one else we can think of did either—was that Xi would add many more titles to create his now very long list of them, eventually becoming, for example, the first CCP leader to be referred to as commander-in-chief.[1])

Our sense of uncertainty while working on the second edition was nothing, however, compared to what we have experienced revising this edition's section on "The Future." Working on it throughout 2017 has proved deeply unsettling, due to the rush of events on both sides of the Pacific Ocean. Most notably, leaving aside its destabilizing impact on the United States, Donald J. Trump's first year in office as president has altered or called into question many features of the international scene

---

1. For a humorous take on Xi's ever-expanding list of titles, see "Badiucao: Xi Jinping's New Business Card," China Digital Times, January 31, 2017, http://chinadigitaltimes.net/2017/01/badiucao-xi-jinpings-new-business-card/ (accessed March 29, 2017).

that previously seemed set in stone. China's relations to the United States, the balance of power within East Asia, and even Xi Jinping's stature as a world leader all seem different than they did twelve months ago.

Even if our publisher had infinite patience and were willing to wait longer for this manuscript, we are not sure that we could pick a specific time in the near future when the dust will have settled. Nothing feels lasting right now, in either the United States or the PRC, and relations between the two countries are similarly in flux—though smoother, on the whole, than many expected at the time that Trump, who was surprisingly popular in China even when lambasting the country on the campaign trail, was elected.[2] In a number of commentaries published immediately after Trump's victory, analysts predicted that tensions in US–China relations would increase under the new president, who during his campaign had frequently promised a trade war with China and appeared scornful of the role the United States had played for decades in maintaining a geopolitical balance in Pacific regional politics.[3] Trump stoked these anxieties several weeks later when he accepted a congratulatory phone call from Taiwan's president, Tsai Ing-wen, breaking a diplomatic script in place since

2. Jiayang Fan has been a thoughtful tracker of shifts in Chinese views of Trump from early in his campaign until the present. See, for example, "The Maoism of Donald Trump," *The New Yorker*, May 13, 2016, https://www.newyorker.com/news/daily-comment/the-maoism-of-donald-trump (accessed November 15, 2017) and her comments on the Sinica Podcast episode "Why Do So Many Chinese People Admire Donald Trump?" June 30, 2016, http://supchina.com/podcast/many-chinese-people-admire-donald-trump/ (accessed November 15, 2017).

3. For a collection of US–China-focused op-eds and analyses published in the days following the 2016 election, see Maura Elizabeth Cunningham, "U.S.-China Relations under Trump: A Reading Round-Up," November 11, 2016, https://mauracunningham.org/2016/11/11/u-s-china-relations-under-trump-a-reading-round-up/ (accessed November 12, 2017).

1979 that dictated no direct contact between the leaders of the United States and Taiwan; Trump subsequently suggested that the "One-China Policy," long a core principle of US–China relations, should be open to re-evaluation. As 2017 began, the relationship between the United States and the PRC, carefully negotiated and nurtured over the past four decades, seemed on the brink of disintegration.

That predicted downward spiral has not materialized, in part because Trump has backed away from the most inflammatory elements of his campaign rhetoric and—in public, at least—has trumpeted his friendly relationship with and admiration for Xi. Shortly after his inauguration, Trump spoke with Xi and assured him that he had no intention of using the One-China Policy as a bargaining chip in US–China relations. The two leaders have hosted each other in reciprocal visits that were much watched for signs of conflict, but were ultimately more tepid than tempestuous, notable more for over-the-top symbolic gestures of goodwill than for substance. As a result of several missile tests in mid-2017, North Korea has replaced China as the greatest threat to the United States in Trump's speeches and tweets. US–China relations may not be their strongest at the moment, and could certainly deteriorate at any time, but as we write this preface in mid-November 2017 the situation is stable, if fragile.

The current stability is not only due to Trump's retreat from his previous China-bashing, but also to Xi's own confidence and strength, both at home and abroad. In the five years since he became the PRC's leader, Xi has taken down his political enemies through an aggressive anti-corruption campaign and silenced dissenting voices through a clampdown on civil society. Government propaganda organs have created a cult of personality around him that is unlike anything seen since the days of Mao Zedong in the 1960s and '70s. At the Nineteenth Party Congress in October 2017, not only was Xi given a predicted second term as general secretary of the CCP, but the party constitution was revised to include a political doctrine named after him, something that had last been done for Deng Xiaoping, and then only posthumously.

While making these authoritarian moves domestically, Xi has simultaneously positioned China as a benevolent global leader seeking only to promote peaceful cooperation and development around the world. His signature foreign policy, the Belt and Road Initiative (called "One Belt, One Road" when it was launched in 2013), provides PRC loans and infrastructure construction knowledge to countries across Eurasia and beyond, creating a regional network of states that are both financially and symbolically indebted to China. In January 2017, Xi became the first top Chinese leader to attend and speak at the Davos World Economic Forum, where his speech celebrated globalization and China's willingness to advance global economic interconnectedness.[4] He followed this up in November 2017 with a similar address at the Asia-Pacific Economic Cooperation (APEC) meeting in Vietnam, again touting the benefits of free trade. At a time when American global leadership is waning, Xi has not hesitated to put China forward as the next leader on the international stage, but one with very different principles and interests. Even though many of his *actions*—from ratcheting up already stringent controls on the Internet to making life increasingly difficult for foreign nongovernmental organizations (NGOs) and many international businesses operating in China—have been those of an economic nationalist, many commentators have given his speeches high marks, welcoming the fact that his *rhetoric* praising rather than criticizing globalization offers such a strong counterpart to what Trump has been saying and tweeting.

Other recent events that make it particularly hard to complete a work on China which strives to be current include the

4. "Full Text of Xi Jinping Keynote at the World Economic Forum," CGTN America, January 17, 2017, http://america.cgtn.com/2017/01/17/full-text-of-xi-jinping-keynote-at-the-world-economic-forum (accessed November 14, 2017).

flurry of new developments within various parts of the PRC. To cite just one case in point, dealing with Hong Kong's shifting political situation in this edition's section on "The Future" would have been complicated even without Trump's ascent. Several worrying events occurred during 2015 and 2016, which flagged the precarious position in which Hong Kong residents who anger the mainland's leaders now find themselves. For example, in late 2015 several booksellers involved in publishing gossipy and lightly sourced works dealing with the private lives of CCP leaders were spirited from Hong Kong, and in one case Thailand, onto the mainland, where some were forced to make televised "confessions" that were clearly coerced. In 2016, Joshua Wong, the most famous leader of 2014's Umbrella Movement (which naturally gets discussed in some detail in this edition), was blocked from speaking in Thailand, presumably because of pressure that Beijing put on Bangkok. That year China's central authorities also intervened in legal procedures in Hong Kong's courts to determine whether elected representatives to the local Legislative Council should be allowed to take their seats or barred from doing so, due to symbolic protests they lodged during oath-taking ceremonies. In 2017, disturbing events have continued to raise concerns about the alarming speed with which the gap separating Hong Kong from mainland urban centers is shrinking. To name just two examples, a British politician with deep ties to the city and a tradition of speaking out about human rights issues was barred from entering Hong Kong, and when Beijing passed a law that made showing disrespect to the national anthem punishable by up to three years in prison, the authorities emphasized that Hong Kong's government would need to find a way of enforcing a form of this regulation inside the city—where booing the song at sporting events has become a popular way of expressing discontent with current political trends.

Too much is happening, and too quickly, for us to assure you that we know where China, or the United States, or US–China relations, are heading. But while we have written this edition's "The Future" chapter with even more uncertainty than we felt while doing the same back in November 2012, we are confident that knowing about China—not only its present, but also its recent and even distant past—remains an essential part of being an engaged citizen in the twenty-first-century world. In this book, we offer the historical, political, and cultural background necessary to see the big picture behind the immediacy of daily news stories. We hope this will assist you in understanding the larger context of those stories—whatever the future may bring.

To keep up with our thinking on current events, please follow us on Twitter: @jwassers and @mauracunningham.

ACKNOWLEDGMENTS

We remain grateful to all of the various publications, institutions, and individuals thanked at the start of the two previous editions, especially our ever-patient editor, Tim Bent. We have also accumulated some new debts, though, in creating this rebooted version of the book. For help with the current edition, we would like to first of all thank Ayesha Saldanha who gave our first draft of this edition a thorough read and made many helpful suggestions to clarify and tighten our writing.

UC Irvine graduate student Kyle David assisted us in getting this project off the ground by reading through the second edition of the book and flagging the sections that should be revised, expanded, or cut altogether. Susan Blumberg-Kason was good enough to review and comment on an early draft of the new question on Hong Kong that appears in chapter 6.

After the second edition of *China in the 21st Century* was published in 2013, we gave several joint talks in China, where audience questions and comments helped us refine our thinking about the country's past and present. Thanks to the Shanghai Foreign Correspondents Club, the Foreign Correspondents' Club of China in Beijing, and the University of Nottingham, Ningbo (where an unnamed student in the audience gets credit for suggesting that the accent color on this edition be green, given the importance of the environment in China) for inviting us to speak. In 2017, the University of Toronto hosted us for a lively discussion about the United States and China in the eras of Trump and Xi. Thanks also to the many other institutions and groups, from the National Committee on US–China Relations to the Hong Kong International Literary Festival and from the CET Study Abroad program to high schools and Boulder's Program for Teaching East Asia, that have invited us to speak solo over the years—there are too many others to list them all, but our interactions with attendees at those events have greatly shaped our understanding of "what everyone needs to know" about China in the twenty-first century.

We are grateful for assistance from the many editors who have helped us, both individually and jointly, improve our writing for non-academic audiences. Liam Fitzpatrick and Zoher Abdoolcarim at *TIME*'s Hong Kong office deserve special mention for their comments and queries on an op-ed we wrote together in early 2017; we also thank editors at the *Los Angeles Review of Books*, *Dissent*, the *Financial Times*, the *Wall Street Journal*, the *Los Angeles Times*, and *World Policy Journal*.

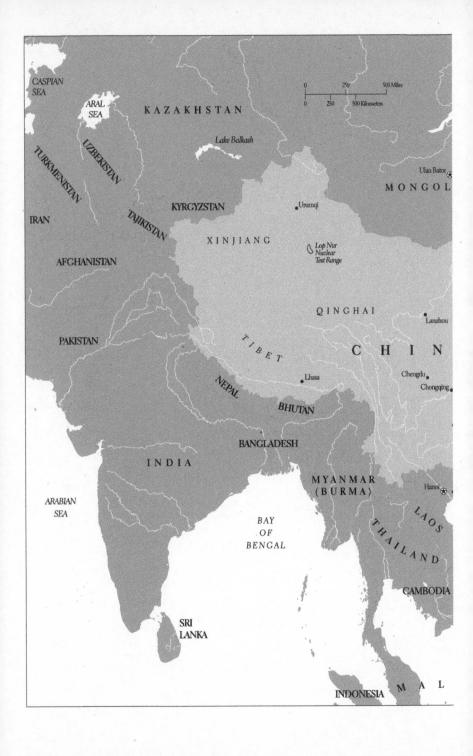

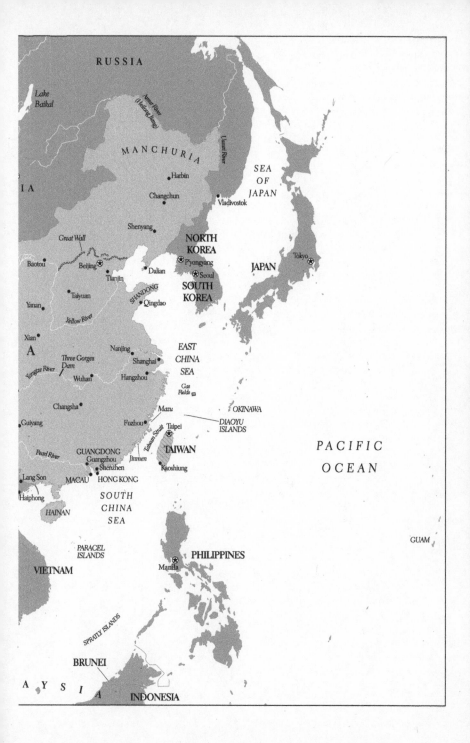

Part I
HISTORICAL LEGACIES

To understand today's China, it is crucial to know something about its past. And especially important for our purposes are those aspects of its history that have direct relevance for contemporary developments, whether because of the precedents they set or because current leaders present themselves as breaking away from them or carrying them forward. With this in mind, and intended to avoid a wearying and confusing march through all the dynasties, the following three chapters offer up a selective (but we hope illuminating) quick run-through of the two millennia-plus that get China from Confucius to Mao.

The first chapter introduces early Chinese schools of thought, especially the ideas of Confucius, since today's leaders seek to depict China as a society where "Confucian" and communist ideals complement one another. It also looks at the place that democratic traditions have had in China, showing that these are not just recent imports from the West. The second chapter focuses on political structures and major political ideas, including the concept of the "Mandate of Heaven," which legitimated imperial rule by asserting a connection between spiritual and earthly dynamics. As well, this chapter examines the similarities and differences in how successive ruling houses, or dynasties, governed China from the third century B.C.E. until 1912, the year that China's last emperor abdicated and a republican form of government was established. Rounding out this first part of the book, chapter 3, "Revolutions and Revolutionaries," looks at the events that transformed the country during the period between 1912 and Mao's death in 1976. It ends with a look at Mao's posthumous legacy, emphasizing the varied ways that the former leader has been perceived in the People's Republic of China (PRC).

1

SCHOOLS OF THOUGHT

Who was Confucius?

Confucius (551–479 B.C.E.) was a teacher and philosopher who lived during the Zhou (Chou[1]) Dynasty (1045–256 B.C.E.), in what is known as the Spring and Autumn Era (722–476 B.C.E.). As with those of his near contemporary Socrates, none of Confucius's writings have survived, and his views come down to us via a text produced after his death.[2] This is the *Analects*, which contains short statements attributed to Confucius (the origins of the "Confucius says" fortune-cookie slips, though these were invented either in Japan in the 1800s or in California in the 1900s) and dialogues between the sage and his disciples.[3] It covers a range of topics, from how a "true gentleman" behaves in his daily life (right down to how he eats with proper decorum) to how a ruler should govern (with a benevolent concern for the well-being of his subjects). One of its most famous statements, linked to both the high value placed on education in Chinese culture and the meritocratic aspect of the Chinese political tradition, is that people are pretty much alike at birth but become differentiated via learning. Another well-known adage from the *Analects* says simply that it is a great pleasure to have friends come to visit from afar.

This last adage gained new fame on August 8, 2008, when it was quoted at the start of the Beijing Games. The line had obvious relevance for the Olympic Opening Ceremony, since the live audience for the grand spectacle held in the Bird's Nest Stadium included foreign leaders, among them George W. Bush (the first sitting American president to attend the Olympics in a foreign country) and Russia's Vladimir Putin. Quoting Confucius also fit with Chinese Olympic publicity efforts generally, which sought to demonstrate that the PRC has become a country that is open to the outside world and respectful of China's ancient traditions and values, while also holding fast to more recent revolutionary ideas.

What were Confucius's core ideas?

The vision of morality sketched out in the *Analects* emphasizes the importance of three things—education, ritual, and relationships—that are hierarchical yet provide benefits to both superior and inferior parties. Education was important because it was by studying the classical texts that a person could learn about and begin to emulate the actions of the most virtuous figures of past ages, including the legendary sages Yao and Shun (who lived long before the founding of the Zhou Dynasty) and figures such as the Duke of Zhou (who lived just a few centuries before Confucius). Ritual, which included a variety of social interactions such as greetings, was important because it was a physical acting-out of the best practices of earlier—and, to Confucius's way of thinking, purer—ages. And relationships in which there was a clear distinction between higher and lower ranks were valued, since in these the responsibilities of each side were clear.

What was his political vision?

Confucius saw political relationships as familial relationships writ large, meaning, for example, that rulers should behave toward those they governed the way that fathers should behave toward their children. He emphasized the importance of four relationships in particular, all of which he saw as reciprocal and all of which he thought involved analogous combinations of benevolence from one party and deference from the other. These relationships were those of ruler and minister (also formulated as ruler and subject), father and son, elder brother and younger brother, and husband and wife. (Later, followers of Confucius added a fifth relationship, more egalitarian than the others: that between friend and friend.)

In each of the four main dyads discussed by Confucius, the former party was expected to protect the latter, and in return the latter was expected to obey the former. The social order was threatened whenever people failed to act according to their prescribed roles.

Confucius lived in a time of civil wars and general instability, which continued during the Warring States era (475–221 B.C.E.) that followed soon after his death. He presented his views as a blueprint that would guarantee that a state would have order within its own borders. He also promised that a ruler who adhered to his teachings would expand the reach of his state, since people living in other kingdoms would flock to such a peaceful, well-governed land.

How important was history to Confucius?

History was crucially important to Confucius. He claimed that the Western Zhou era (1046–770 B.C.E.) had been a golden age of harmony and enlightened rulers and called on people to study that age, which he lauded as a time when people knew their proper places within the social order. According to the *Analects*, the first thing that a true ruler could do to improve the present was to honor the past and revive the rituals and even the music of the Western Zhou, as a means to encourage proper deportment. This ruler should also ensure that his own behavior toward his subjects was a model of paternal benevolence at all moments, since this would lead to emulation by all others in a comparably superior position. A land with a good ruler would inevitably be one with good fathers (and other lineage elders) and good husbands.

There was a self-serving side to this argument. For to accomplish these things, Confucius and his followers claimed, it would serve the true king well to rely upon advisers who were thoroughly versed in classical works and had made a specialty of studying the ways of the past. In other words, Confucius and his followers suggested that rulers heed the advice of scholarly specialists in ritual such as themselves.

Was Confucius celebrated in his own times?

The sage was not particularly successful in gaining followers in his own lifetime. He would occasionally win the ear of a ruler, but never had the opportunity he sought of being a long-term adviser to one. And things did not improve dramatically in the centuries immediately following his death in 479 B.C.E., though significant refinements of and additions to his thought were made during that time by such figures as Mencius (372–289 B.C.E.), second in importance only to Confucius in the development of what would later become known as Confucianism (the notion that their ideas constituted a clearly defined creed, comparable to a Western religion, was a much later invention).[4] Up until the end of the Warring States period in the second century B.C.E, in fact, Confucius's ideas were still but one school of thought, others being Daoism (Taoism), Legalism, and a host of now-obscure creeds that were occasionally embraced by one or another ruler of the many competing kingdoms that made up what we now call China. Even when Confucius's teachings took hold, it was often in a diluted form, combined with aspects of competing schools.

The proponents of some rival schools of thought, moreover, scoffed at Confucius and his beliefs. He was sometimes mocked by Daoists, who took a more egalitarian view of social relations than did the followers of Confucius and prized spontaneity over rituals. Legalists insisted that rulers should not strive to be admired for their virtues but rather take steps to ensure that they were respected and feared for the way they distributed rewards and punishments. The Daoists and Legalists, though disagreeing with one another on many things, agreed that the emphasis Confucius put on the study of dusty classics was misguided. The former thought it wrong because the golden age they admired was the Shang Dynasty (c. 1600–1046 B.C.E.), an era of simplicity that preceded the creation of Zhou texts. The latter, a group of pragmatists, argued that rulers should adapt to the challenges of each new age.

As late as 221 B.C.E., when several of the embattled kingdoms of the Warring States were brought under the control of the head of the kingdom of Qin (Ch'in), it was still far from clear that Confucius would end up the most influential of early philosophers. The founder of the Qin Dynasty (221–206 B.C.E.), who became known to posterity as China's first emperor, had no time for Confucian ideas. He favored the Legalists, who told him how to maximize his authority, rather than the scholars, who told him how to behave benevolently. Qin Shi Huang, the first emperor, is now remembered (correctly) for the Terracotta Army built to serve him after death, and (incorrectly) for creating the Great Wall of China. While he did build some large fortifications, the sites tourists visit today and are described as dating back to Qin Shi Huang's time actually tend to be remnants of a much later wall-building dynasty, that of the Ming (1368–1644).[5] Yet the legend that Qin Shi Huang created the Great Wall is believable because the Legalist ideas he embraced enabled him to summon huge armies of laborers on demand.

The few accounts written near the lifetime of the first emperor, all crafted by historians serving the next dynasty, present Qin Shi Huang as a cruel despot.[6] In these works, he is described as a model of how not to rule and as someone so hated by his subjects that the dynasty he had dreamed would go on for centuries was instead overthrown by a popular rebellion that broke out soon after his death, just as his son's reign was beginning. (The Qin did leave one enduring legacy, as the dynasty's name helped lead to China being called "China," a term that sounds nothing like the primary Chinese terms for the country, such as "Zhongguo," meaning "Middle Kingdom.") As a result of the Qin Dynasty's brief hold on power, while one can find traces of Legalist influence in the belief systems of many later dynasties, the creed was almost never officially endorsed after the Han Dynasty (206 B.C.E.–220 C.E.) was founded.

When did the ideas of Confucius gain influence?

It was not until the Qin Dynasty had fallen and the Han Dynasty established that the ideas of Confucius became a core part of official ideology. And even then, Confucianism was combined with elements drawn from other schools of thought, such as Daoism and the Yin-Yang line of cosmological thinking, which emphasizes the interconnectedness of things that seem clearly different or even opposite; it was sometimes regarded as simply a part of the Daoist creed, but was at other times viewed as its own school of thought.

Confucian ideals and practices were extolled by most successive dynasties, though they were often, as in the Han period, braided together with concepts and rituals taken from other creeds. These included Daoism (always a presence) and Chinese folk religious traditions. In addition, Confucianism was eventually influenced greatly by ideas associated with the imported but quickly domesticated belief system of Buddhism, which reached an early point of high influence in China during the Tang (T'ang) Dynasty (618–907 C.E.), a cosmopolitan era when many ideas and objects flowed in through overland trade routes such as the Silk Road. Buddhist concepts were crucial in contributing to modifications within the Confucian tradition during the Song (Sung) Dynasty (960–1279) that were so significant that the term "neo-Confucianism" is used to describe them.

What was the status of Confucianism to 1949?

From the Han Dynasty onward, Confucian ideas remained central to Chinese political practices regardless of which dynasty was in power, until a dramatic dip in Confucius's fortunes came in the early 1900s. Many Chinese intellectuals of the time argued that an attachment to Confucian values was responsible for the country's decline. They blamed Confucius for China's position of backwardness vis-à-vis the West and Japan, a formerly Confucian country that had begun to embrace European and American ways in the mid-nineteenth century.

The most disruptive pre-1949 anti-Confucian upsurge occurred during the New Culture movement, which began in 1915 and lasted until the mid-1920s. This was an iconoclastic struggle that one leader, Hu Shi (Hu Shih; 1891–1962), a student of the American philosopher John Dewey, would describe as "the Chinese Renaissance" in a book by that title based on lectures he gave in Chicago in the 1930s. The Chinese Renaissance also had things in common with the Enlightenment (its radical questioning of tradition and prizing of rationality) and the Western counterculture movement of the 1960s (its extolling the value of youth, for example, and its celebration of new forms of art and literature).[7]

Participants in the New Culture movement, including a young Mao Zedong (Mao Tse-tung; 1893–1976) and the great Chinese writer Zhou Shuren (Chou Hsu-ren; 1881–1936), who published under the pen name Lu Xun (Lu Hsün), wrote scathingly about how Confucius had shaped a China in which age was venerated at the expense of youth, women were repressed, individualism and creativity were stifled, and a cult of tradition prevented innovation. To join the modern world, they argued, China needed to jettison Confucius and everything he represented, embracing the best that the West had to offer as Japan had done—resulting in its rise in global influence. They also insisted that intellectuals stop using classical

Chinese, which was far removed from vernacular forms of communication, and develop a "plain speech" (*baihua*) form of writing to take its place.

Some New Culture veterans would stick to anti-Confucian positions for decades. Others would eventually abandon them, throwing their lot in with the Nationalist Party, which began as a radical revolutionary group but later became a conservative political organization.

Under the leadership of Chiang Kai-shek (Jiang Jieshi; 1887–1975), the Nationalists of the 1930s would, in fact, be responsible for a major Confucian revival. Chiang insisted that China's best route forward was to find a way to combine Confucian values with the most advanced technologies and best ideas coming from Japan and the West. Despite being a Christian, Chiang elevated the Chinese sage's birthday to the status of a state holiday. He argued that the emphasis on tradition, family, social order, and clearly delineated hierarchies in Confucianism could go hand in hand with the teachings of the Bible.

Is Confucianism a religion?

Confucius himself was more of a philosophical than a religious figure. Even though his emphasis on looking up to elders fit in well with the practices of ancestor worship, which predated his time and remained a mainstay of Chinese tradition, his teachings offered no details about an afterlife.

Nevertheless, throughout Chinese history, he has occasionally been elevated to a saintlike status, with temples being devoted to him (including some that have recently been spruced up by the government) and his Shandong Province hometown of Qufu being transformed into a pilgrimage site (with, lately, a bit of a theme-park aspect thrown in). Ironically, the period of rule by the Christian Chiang Kai-shek was a time in which Confucius was revered, as is the current era of rule by the allegedly atheist Communist Party.

Many non-Chinese have argued that the country has three major religions: Confucianism, Daoism, and Buddhism. Though Confucianism is more a philosophy than a religion, Daoism and Buddhism are indeed important systems of belief in China. Yet religious identity is more fluid than in the Judeo-Christian West, as many Chinese will move, sometimes unconsciously, among the three practices depending on context. Someone, for example, might worship at a Confucian temple right before an important school exam (due to the sage's association with learning) but also consider him- or herself a practicing Buddhist, adhering to a vegetarian diet and reciting sutras every morning. Buddhism, like all other religions, was suppressed during the Mao era, but it has enjoyed a popular revival in recent decades. Like Confucian temples, many Buddhist ones have recently been renovated and, sometimes, turned into tourist destinations where people can observe "releasing life" ceremonies (at which live fish and birds are released into the wild), walk through a restored temple complex, have lunch at a vegetarian restaurant, and finish their visit with a trip to the gift shop to purchase incense sticks and bracelets of prayer beads.

How did Confucius fare during the Mao years?

Not surprisingly, when the Chinese Communist Party (CCP) took power on October 1, 1949, after driving Chiang into exile on Taiwan, it immediately put an end to the celebrations of Confucius's birthday that had been held during the years of Nationalist rule. The official line on the sage throughout the Mao years (1949–1976)—as the first decades of CCP rule are often called—was that he had done China far more harm than good. Criticism of the man, his ideas, and his legacy peaked in the early 1970s, with the launch of a mass campaign aimed at ridding the country of all lingering Confucian influence. In posters, pamphlets, and speeches Confucius was excoriated as an evil figure whose hide-bound, anti-egalitarian ideas had done great damage to generations of Chinese men and even more damage to Chinese women. He was blamed for having supported a wide range of unjust and immoral practices, from ancestor worship to viewing daughters as less valuable than sons, which had kept China in a "feudal" (*fengjian*) state for millennia.

The first decades of Communist rule may have been a time when egalitarian values were celebrated, but new forms of inequality took root, as CCP cadres emerged as a class with special privileges. During the Mao years, the government worked to eradicate Confucian beliefs that had become deeply embedded in Chinese society. It minimized the importance of the family as a social unit by establishing collectives and communes, and China's leadership stressed working toward a bright new future over celebrating a past golden age. It was also one of those rare times in Chinese history when Legalism was sometimes viewed in a positive way. Mao was fond of saying that China's first emperor—with his Legalist ideas, disdain for book-learning detached from pragmatic concerns, and ability to get big things done—was among the best.

How has Confucius fared since Mao's death?

In the immediate wake of Mao's death in September 1976, Confucius's reputation did not change dramatically. Mao was succeeded as chairman by Hua Guofeng (Hua Kuo-feng; 1921–2008), whom he had allegedly hand-picked to follow him, but who didn't enjoy widespread CCP support. Hua served as a kind of place-holder, continuing Mao's policies for a few years before being pushed to the side by Deng Xiaoping (Teng Hsiao-p'ing; 1904–1997). Hua spent the last decades of his life occupying relatively minor official posts. Criticism of Confucius diminished during the almost two decades that Deng was the most powerful man in China, and by the turn of the century, the balance had tipped decisively back toward Confucius.

You would not have known about these post-1949 ups and downs given the celebratory way Confucius was treated during the 2008 Olympics. Not only did the opening ceremony begin with a quote from the *Analects*, a modern-day member of the Kong lineage that claims Confucius as an ancestor (the foreign term "Confucius" is derived from Kong Zi, or Master Kong) played a symbolically important role in the pre-games torch run. During the opening ceremony, three thousand performers dressed as the sage's disciples—all of whom, incidentally, belonged to the People's Liberation Army (PLA)—paraded through the Bird's Nest Stadium as President Hu Jintao (1942–) smiled down on them. This was meant to suggest that for millennia (and presumably without interruption), Confucius had been a kind of national saint for China.

Displays of this kind would have been impossible to imagine back in Mao's day, but Western television broadcasters didn't comment on this contrast. Instead, the announcers tended to simply follow the script provided to them by the official Xinhua (New China) News Agency and refer to the respectful treatment of Confucius as a natural expression of China's reverence for the traditions and great men of the country's past.

Why is Confucius back in favor?

The renewal of official veneration of Confucius, though representing an about-face for the CCP, fits in with a general tendency by several recent leaders, including current head of both party and state Xi Jinping (1953–), to emphasize continuity with the past. Official statements boast of the country's glorious "five thousand years" of "unbroken" cultural development, and make references to China being the "only unified and continuous civilization" in the modern world.[8] This assertion is a problematic one, given how many changes over time there have been in China's borders and the values and traditions of the people living within them. Nevertheless, a mix-and-match approach to history is now the order of the day, in which anything that suggests past greatness is held up as worthy of respect.

The image of today's China as carrying forward elements of its distant past involves not just Confucius but other figures and symbols linked to early periods of history. This is true even of sites that were previously seen as reminders of the failings rather than the glories of the past. For example, Mao did not treat the Forbidden City as sacred, allowing this home of the emperors of China's last two dynasties, the Ming and the Qing (Ch'ing; 1644–1911), to fall into disrepair. The grounds contained sculptures that drew attention to the unjust ways that ordinary Chinese were treated by rulers and landlords in the dark period before the communist revolution. Now, however, the old palace complex has been carefully restored and is presented as a symbol of the glamour and beauty—not decadence—of the past. Visiting dignitaries are given tours that extoll the glories of the country's artistic and architectural traditions.

No longer is it a matter of choosing between celebrating the words of Confucius or the deeds of the first emperor. The *Analects* and the Terracotta Warriors are now treated as complementary rather than competing symbols of ancient China's glory.

This pairing of ancient icons fits in with the desire of China's current leaders to cultivate national pride by presenting the country as one that was great in the past and has become so again on their watch. Moreover, it encourages people of Chinese descent in Taiwan, Australia, the United States, and other parts of the world (even those with no love for communism) to identify with, travel to, and invest in the PRC.

There are also more specific reasons that Confucius is back. There was a good fit, for example, between the emphasis that Confucius and his followers have always placed on social order and the focus that Hu Jintao had placed on the themes of "harmony" and stability in his speeches. Xi Jinping's talk

of realizing a long-held "Chinese Dream" of "national rejuvenation," as well as his call for rejection of Western values and
ideas—presumably excepting, of course, those associated with
one thinker from the West, Karl Marx—also fit in with elevation of the best-known traditional Chinese philosopher to a
venerated status.

Mao, in keeping with Marxist tradition, stressed that progress is made via class conflict. By contrast, China's recent
leaders have all claimed that while they still adhere to Marxism
the country can best move forward if all people within it work
together. The vision they want pursued is not one achieved
via struggle, but by unifying around the objectives of development and "harmonious society" (*hexie shehui*), a goal identified
with Hu that remains a focus under his successor, Xi.

There was a moment during the Olympics Opening
Ceremony when the contours of the Hu catchphrase's main
character, *he* (harmony), were visually displayed in an eye-
catching manner. The list of fifty officially approved slogans
for the large parade held on October 1, 2009, to mark the six-
tieth birthday of the PRC included several with *hexie*, one of
which called on the people to help the CCP "build a socialist
harmonious society and promote social equity and justice." Xi,
while bringing in new slogans of his own, continues to refer to
China being best served by various kinds of *he*, including that
between religious and social groups.[9]

How has Confucius been used in recent years?

In addition to sanctioning the sage's appearance during the
Olympics and echoing the *Analects* and later Confucian texts
in calls for "harmonious" social relations, the Chinese government has sponsored the creation and funding of approximately five hundred Confucius Institutes around the world
since 2004. These are modeled in part on the German Goethe
Institutes, and their stated intent is to further understanding
of China's cultural legacy via activities, such as classes in the

Chinese language and courses on Chinese history that empha-size continuities with the past and the "five thousand years of Chinese civilization" idea. However, as many scholars and journalists have stressed, one key contrast with the Goethe Institutes is that Confucius Institutes, unlike their more inde-pendent German counterparts, are funded by and answer di-rectly to the Chinese Ministry of Education.[10]

As a result of their government connections, Confucius Institutes have sometimes sparked controversies, including several in the United States. Some commentators have suggested that they are part of a Chinese plot to infiltrate US communities. Pointing to the fact that institute money and personnel come from a ministry within the PRC government, such alarmism harks back to the Red Scare of the 1950s. There is, though, a much more sensible basis for concern. Namely, some scholars worry that a university with funding coming from an arm of the Beijing government could end up curtailing intellectual freedom on campus, perhaps in subtle ways. For example, Chinese authorities often express displeasure when foreign officials and institutions host the Dalai Lama. It is easy to imagine a university planning to honor him hearing overt or veiled threats from the Chinese government suggesting that, among other things, this might lead to Confucius Institute funding being withdrawn from the school. Sometimes, rep-resentatives of the Chinese government are invited to attend campus speaker series supported by Confucius Institutes, so it is also possible that organizers of these series might steer clear of inviting foreign scholars with particularly close ties to dissidents-in-exile or mainland political prisoners to be part of these events, simply to minimize the chance for any awkward-ness on the part of a patron.

Such concerns have led some universities to reject offers from the Chinese government to establish a Confucius Institute at their school. Others, most notably the University of Chicago and Pennsylvania State University, have declined to renew their Confucius Institutes at the end of their initial five-year contracts. Although these decisions were generally viewed with favor by faculty, those schools did not cite questions of academic freedom as the official cause for closure; rather, they expressed displeasure with the narrow mandate and rigid conditions of the partnership.[11]

What is too rarely noted in commentaries on these Confucius Institutes is that, given the anti-Confucius stance of the CCP under Mao, Beijing's choice of nomenclature is shocking to those with a sense of history. It would be as though Moscow under the Soviets had set up "Tsar Nicholas Institutes" to spread understanding of Russian culture around the world.

Today's revival of official Confucianism is one of the many echoes that reverberate from the era of Chiang Kai-shek.[12] Now, as then, the leader of a party once associated with revolution and upheaval is drawing inspiration from a philosopher who championed tradition and harmony. This renascence of Confucianism has led to the restoration of temples and erection of statues devoted to Confucius; indeed, in some parts of China, Confucius statues now outnumber those of Mao. The government has taken steps to make Qufu a major draw for both Chinese tourists and visitors from other countries with Confucian heritages, such as South Korea and Japan.

Though the initiatives described above are all government-led, there has also been a popular revival of interest in Confucius. One of the best-selling nonfiction books published in the PRC during the first decade of this century was a work on the *Analects* by the academic-turned-media-personality Yu Dan. This bestseller, a kind of *Chicken Soup for the Soul* with Chinese characteristics, has been criticized for bowdlerizing the ideas of Confucius. Nevertheless, Yu's book (also available in English) sold more than four million copies during the six months following its 2006 publication and remains popular.[13]

The government has hailed the Yu Dan phenomenon as evidence of the complementary nature of the longing for social harmony by both the people and the regime. One could, though, see it as part of a deeper hunger among disillusioned people for something new to believe in—even if that something new is something very old repackaged in a novel way.

Yet the PRC regime has subtly walked back its sponsorship of Confucius since the Olympics in a couple of ways. One of the oddest incidents involving the sage occurred in January 2011, when a thirty-one-foot-tall statue of Confucius was installed in Tiananmen Square, China's most symbolically fraught public space. In April, however, the massive statue disappeared overnight. It had been moved to a courtyard within the National Museum, just off the square, for reasons that still remain unclear.[14] Although Xi, like Hu, sometimes uses terms that call Confucius to mind, he has shown more of an interest than his predecessor in promoting the classics in general. He not only cites Confucius in speeches but other ancient thinkers, including Han Feizi, a philosopher linked to the competing school of Legalism.[15]

Did Confucianism hinder imperial China's economic development?

The influential German social theorist Max Weber, for one, certainly thought Confucianism hindered imperial China's economic development. According to Weber, while Protestantism encouraged the sort of innovation and concern with transformation that drives capitalism, the emphasis Confucius put on recapturing the glories of past times was a brake on development. In addition, Confucian texts claimed that aside from the ruling family there were four basic social groups in China. The two most valuable ones in the eyes of Confucius and his followers were scholars (who made sure that the country was well governed) and farmers (who provided it with food); of lesser value were artisans (who were not essential but made products that were useful); and least valued of all—indeed, despised—were the merchants (who did not contribute to the good of the community at all).

There are two problems, however, with thinking of Confucianism as a block on economic development.

First, as work by economic historians has shown, as late as 1750 the most economically vibrant parts of Confucian China during the Qing dynasty were roughly as commercialized and prosperous as the most economically vibrant parts of Protestant Europe. Factors other than modes of thought thus need to be seen as leading to what has been termed the "great divergence" between Western and Chinese economic development after that point.[16] Other things that made a difference included the distribution of natural resources (England was lucky to have large coal supplies located in parts of the country that were close to its commercial centers, for example) and the various forms that imperialism took, with European empires expanding overseas. According to this research, Britain's extraordinary takeoff had much to do with the fact it could make use of land-intensive products from overseas facilitated by the legacies of slavery and colonialism, and compensating for Europe's relatively low agricultural yields per acre. The country also had domestic coal deposits that were relatively easy to access; although the Qing had plenty of areas to mine, they were in regions that were hard to reach before the era of railroads.

Secondly, many of the economic success stories of recent decades have involved East Asian countries that, like China, were influenced greatly by Confucianism. After the rapid takeoff of Japan, Hong Kong, South Korea, Singapore, and Taiwan, the notion that Confucian values stand in the way of capitalism seems untenable.

There is also the fact that today's China, while not exactly capitalist—some 70 percent of the top five hundred companies in the PRC are state-owned, and much of its overall wealth is in the form of government assets—has experienced a great economic boom. That this transpired in an era of renewed celebration of Confucius, even a symbolic one, is another nail in the Weberian conceptual coffin.

Indeed, in the wake of recent economic shifts, some have turned Weber upside down and claimed that while Confucian thinkers may have dismissed merchants as unproductive, the kind of family-centered and generally collectivist and cooperative approach to life fostered by Confucianism is conducive to certain forms of highly profitable business activities. Whether or not this is true, the idea that people who share "Confucian" values, however defined, are naturally well disposed to do business with one another seems pertinent. The largest investors in joint enterprises with the Chinese state have tended to be companies based in neighboring countries, including Taiwan, that see themselves as sharing a cultural bond, partly via Confucius, with the PRC.

Does China have an indigenous "democratic" tradition?

Chinese modes of thought are sometimes described as particularly well suited to authoritarianism, and the emphasis on hierarchy and deference within Confucianism and on harsh punishments within Legalism lend credence to this notion. And yet, some elements of China's multi-stranded intellectual tradition are more democratic than authoritarian.[17]

For example, as already noted, Daoist classics encourage people to view hierarchical relationships with skepticism and question whether those in positions of superiority are any better than or different from anyone else. This is not a "democratic" notion in the sense that it calls for elections, but it does provide a basis for challenging rather than accepting power relations within a society.

In addition, even within the Confucian tradition, there is a democratic strand. This is linked to the concept, not exclusively Confucian but certainly associated with Confucianism, of the "Mandate of Heaven" (Tianming) as the basis for political authority. The idea here is that emperors were the earthly representation of Heaven (Tian), a depersonalized spiritual force whose role in running the universe was comparable to that of the emperor's role on earth (literally, *Tianxia*, or "the realm of all under Heaven").

Heaven offered a mandate (*ming*) to each new dynasty, according to this view, but this right to govern was revocable. If an emperor failed to carry out his role correctly, Heaven could transfer the mandate to a new ruler.

Mencius provided the most elaborate early vision of the workings of this process. He claimed that rulers deserved to govern only so long as they demonstrated a true affection for the people and protected their interests. This complemented the emphasis in the *Analects* on the ruler being like a father to his subjects. Mencius went so far as to claim that rulers who failed to behave benevolently toward those below them in the social order forfeited their right to be treated deferentially.

In one famous formulation (found in *Mencius*, Book V, Part A), he stated that while rulers govern by virtue of a "Heavenly Mandate" (*Tianming*), they should remember that, according to the ancient *Book of Documents* (*Shu Jing*): "Heaven sees with the eyes of its people. Heaven hears with the ears of its people." This meant that if the people, with good cause, were thoroughly dissatisfied, Heaven would naturally find it suitable to stop protecting the emperor and would add its support to those seeking to establish a new dynasty. In such a case, rebellion was both likely and morally justified.

This is, again, not an argument for elections, which those of us living in the West and some other countries (India, for example) tend to equate with democracy. Still, it is an important expression of a kind of democratic sentiment.

What does the Chinese term for democracy mean exactly?

The standard Chinese term for democracy is *minzhu*, which, like many complex concepts, is composed of two characters with separate meanings. *Min* means people, while *zhu* means rule.

This compound word, like the original Greek term for democracy (which has a parallel etymology tied to people and rule), can be interpreted in various ways. It can conjure images of direct rule by the masses, or imply simply that the best government is led by a ruler who pays close attention to the interests of the population at large. There is another interpretation of *minzhu* that has long been popular among some highly educated Chinese. This might be called representative democracy sans elections, or the idea that intellectuals should advise rulers to ensure that the interests of the people are respected.

One basis for this idea, which is linked to the emphasis Confucius put on learning, is that from Han times onward civil service examinations were used to fill many government positions. The use of tests that required mastery of Confucian precepts for those seeking high office became particularly important after the expansion of the system during the Song Dynasty (960–1279). By no means did emperors always heed the counsel of intellectuals, but the idea that intellectuals are natural spokespeople for the masses took root and has endured.

If the government's promotion of Confucianism represents one kind of reworking of an old idea to further a twenty-first-century mission, efforts by artists and intellectuals to represent the current regime as morally bankrupt and to call for change in the name of the people represent another. Both proponents of the current order and those fighting to change the way China is governed can tap into elements of the country's multi-stranded intellectual and political traditions.

2

IMPERIAL CHINA

What were the main early dynasties?

A standard way to break up Chinese history is to start with 221 B.C.E., the year that Qin Shi Huang transformed various small states into something big enough to qualify as an empire. There were earlier dynasties ruling part or all the land just north and just south of the Yellow River, which comprise the heartland of what we now call China and where many capital cities, including the present one, Beijing, have stood.

The earliest of these ancient dynasties was the Xia (Hsia; 2070–1600 B.C.E.), often viewed as a mythic entity since there is little reliable evidence to show that it even existed. Next came the Shang (c. 1600–c. 1046 B.C.E.), whose rituals of state included the use of oracle bones (animal parts used for divination), some of which have been unearthed. Oracle bones contain writing that can be linked to the characters that were used in classical texts, which eventually became the building blocks of modern Chinese. Following this came the Zhou (1046–256 B.C.E.), whose early years in power Confucius—as discussed in chapter 1—extolled as a golden age. None of these dynasties controlled nearly as great a territory as the Qin.[1]

The leader of the rebellion that toppled the Qin in 206 B.C.E. became the first emperor of the Han Dynasty, which would transform China into a much larger country and, as we have seen, was the first to give the ideas of Confucius a central part in state ideology. The Han period of rule and expansion was roughly contemporaneous with and similar in some ways to the Roman Age in the West.

The Han historian Sima Qian (Ssu-Ma Ch'ien; c. 145 or 135–86 B.C.E.), China's first great writer of history and often still considered the preeminent Chinese chronicler, repudiated the activities of the Qin. Nevertheless, in the first of many ironies of this kind, the Han left in place basic elements of the political system that Qin Shi Huang had created, including the use of a civil bureaucracy differentiated from the military, a key Qin innovation. One indication of just how important the Han period was is that, while the term "Qin" helped provide a name for the country, the name of the following dynasty was taken as the shorthand for the land's inhabitants. The majority population of the PRC is dubbed the Han, and official statistical counts place nine out of ten citizens of the country in this broadly defined ethnic group (more on that below).

How did dynasties rule?

One enduring feature of the Chinese imperial system was the special status of the emperor as both a religious and political figure who performed ritual functions as an intermediary between *Tian* (Heaven) and *Tianxia* (the human world). Another enduring feature was the central political role played not just by the monarch but also by members of his family (and, rarely, *her* family; with only a couple of exceptions, the ruler of imperial China was male).

In China's imperial system, in contrast to many other monarchies, the successor to the emperor was not necessarily his eldest son. As a result, intense political maneuvering before and immediately after a ruler's death was common.

In addition, since the emperor often had children with more than one wife and one or more concubines, the stakes of succession were great for a large number of people. And there were many mothers, uncles, aunts, and so forth of a monarch or monarch-to-be who could wield influence, especially since close family members were sometimes appointed regents of young successors to the throne.

The most powerful people in imperial China, other than members of the ruling family, tended to be either scholar-officials or eunuchs. The former group included ministers of state, provincial governors, and the crucially important local magistrates, who fulfilled at the county level a mixture of ritual and political roles comparable to those the emperor performed for the entire empire.

Having only eunuchs as servants and banning men capable of impregnating royal wives and concubines from residing in imperial residences ensured order within the imperial household; thus, in this realm, the potential for disputes over the paternity of potential heirs was minimized. The highest-ranking bureaucrats were always supposed to be more powerful than any eunuch, but due to their special access to the emperor and other members of the royal family, eunuchs sometimes wielded the greatest influence. When dynasties were criticized for becoming corrupt, eunuchs were often blamed—though, in a misogynist vein, imperial decline was also sometimes attributed to the nefarious behind-the-scenes workings of palace women, from mothers of young emperors to the scheming concubines of elderly male rulers.[2]

What was the "dynastic cycle"?

The concept of the dynastic cycle held that one dynasty should periodically give way to another. The founders of dynasties (whether rebels who succeeded or the leaders of foreign armies who seized the country) could come to power, according to this line of thought, only because Heaven saw them as virtuous and deserving to rule. Over time, however, their descendants were likely to become less mindful of the people's needs, a variation on the Western adage that power corrupts. The political order would then need to be purified through transfer of the mandate to a new group. This would restart the cycle of virtuous founder and decadent descendants.

Because the natural and the political worlds were viewed as analogous to and in sync with one another, indications that the Mandate of Heaven had been lost by the current leader and was ready to be claimed by a new one included unusual events, such as natural disasters. Eclipses could also be interpreted as signals of Heaven's displeasure about some occurrence in the human world. Emperors, therefore, wanted to know when these would take place, in order to be prepared to offer the people a suitable interpretation of the event.

What were the political implications of this cyclical view?

In contrast to monarchical orders in which every new ruler can trace descent to a common ancestor (e.g., the current Japanese emperor claims to be part of the same lineage as the first one), an order in which there were occasional shifts in rulers was assumed to be a good thing.

Bureaucrats and ministers, who generally attained their posts by passing rigorous civil-service exams rather than by inheriting their positions à la European aristocrats, faced a tough choice whenever rebellions started or foreign armies threatened the state. They had to decide whether or not the current ruling house had lost the Mandate of Heaven, and whether or not, in guarding the interests of the people, they should switch sides.

Finally, since new dynasties often maintained their predecessors' institutions, there was considerable continuity. A new dynasty often relied heavily upon officials who had served the previous dynasty and then jumped ship to join the new one.

Did all dynasties govern in the same way?

Despite the continuities listed so far, there were always important variations among dynasties, with each leaving its distinct
mark, meaning that putting too much emphasis on the idea
of dynastic cycles can distort our sense of the disparate nature of China's past. One basic difference among dynasties is
that they governed territories of radically varying sizes. A map
of today's PRC shows borders defining China that came into
being only after the Qing Dynasty had engaged in many
decades of imperial expansion after taking power in 1644.

Even some very significant dynasties governed territories
much smaller than this. Consider, for instance, that the Song
(960–1279), who ruled a land mass less than half the size of
the PRC, not only oversaw the institutionalization of the civil
service system but also governed during a period of economic
development so dramatic that some scholars locate the start of
modern China in that period.

The Ming Dynasty (1368–1644) had a larger domain than
the Song. But Ming emperors did not control Tibet, the mountainous region far west of the Yellow River heartland that
the PRC claims has been part of China for many centuries.
Nor did the Ming empire include Xinjiang, the region in the
northwestern corner of the PRC whose name (the characters
for it mean "New Frontier") refers to its late incorporation
into the Chinese empire, accomplished via a succession of
Qing Dynasty military campaigns that began in the seven-
teenth century and did not fully conclude until the end of the
nineteenth.

Just as there were dynasties that sometimes failed to govern
lands that are now considered part of China, there were also
emperors who ruled territory that is no longer part of the PRC.
Vietnam, for instance, was sometimes but not always part of
the Chinese empire before the twentieth century.

In addition, dynasties that came to power via wars of conquest took on the roles of the rulers they displaced but always
modified the system they inherited. This was especially true

of dynasties that had their ethnic and cultural roots on the steppes of Central and Northeastern Asia, in regions such as Mongolia and Manchuria that were to the north of and less agricultural than the Chinese heartland.

Under Kublai Khan (1215–1294) and other rulers of the Yuan Dynasty (1271–1368), for example, Confucian civil-service exams were suspended. And the early Manchu emperors of the Qing wrote some documents in their native language and some documents in Chinese.

The Qing set up a dual-track official system in which some posts were reserved for ethnic Manchus, while others were given to members of the Han ethnic group, to which the majority of people living south of the Great Wall belonged. The Qing also maintained special troops (the Banner forces), composed only of people who traced their descent from the northern steppes.

Was the status of women the same under all dynasties?

Shifts in the status of women—or the lack thereof—offer further evidence for the need to think about variations as well as continuities across dynasties. Modern observers, both within China and outside the country, criticize Confucianism for creating a patriarchy that oppressed women in imperial China. Yet women had very different experiences depending on the time, place, ethnic group, and social class in which they were born. It is therefore impossible to generalize about the status of women in traditional China—although the historical records that have survived mostly tell us about the lives of women who belonged to the upper classes.

During the Tang Dynasty (618–907 C.E.), for example, elite women participated in society and enjoyed a higher degree of autonomy compared to women in the Song Dynasty that followed. The Song, a time of Confucian revival, saw the spread of foot-binding and the confinement of women to the home. Yet although they were physically more restricted, elite

Song women were generally literate, possessed greater property rights than women who came before or after them, and also took an active role in arranging the marriages of their children.[3]

Upper-class women who lived during the Ming and Qing dynasties cultivated their skills in writing, needlework, and music, many of them becoming highly accomplished in these arts of the domestic sphere. Very few women questioned the social structures that kept them tied to the home while men controlled China's political, legal, educational, and economic institutions. (Although the idea that women remained at home while men went out into the world divides things too neatly; plenty of elite women traveled.) In their own ways, elite Ming and Qing women carved out spaces for themselves, creating vibrant intellectual, cultural, and social networks.[4]

As noted, the examples above all focus on the experiences of upper-class women; servants, courtesans, widows, and impoverished women lived within many more social and economic constraints. This is also not to overstate the agency of women in imperial China, but to point out that the common narrative about women's victimization under Confucianism needs more nuance. The status of women varied considerably with time and place, and seemingly rigid Confucian ideology often proved more fluid in practice as both men and women adapted to political, economic, and social changes.

How did dynasties interact with foreign countries?

One shared characteristic of most dynasties was that Chinese emperors thought of their domain as the most important in the entire world. Partly because Confucian thought emphasized clear hierarchies, the emperors expected heads of other states to treat them with deference, in return offering these entities protection and benevolence.

Nevertheless, the way that individual dynasties dealt with the outside world varied. During the Tang Dynasty, for example, Chinese links to other regions were especially robust, due to steady movement of people, products, and cultural forms across Eurasia via a loosely defined set of land routes that a nineteenth-century explorer would dub the Silk Road. The enduring power of this evocative name helps explain why Chinese leaders have named current efforts to ramp up ties to other countries the Belt and Road Initiative (about which more below). The latter half of this term conjures up images of a return to the era of the Tang, though there are other aspects of that period, including the relatively high status of women, that differ dramatically from the current one.[5]

Just as dynasties differed from one another when it came to engagement with the wider world, so, too, did individual rulers. Some were much more open to imported ideas and more involved in international trade and exploration than were others. There were Ming emperors, for example, who welcomed Jesuits from Europe, partly because Western advances in astronomy were helpful in predicting eclipses. It was also a Ming emperor who funded the fabled naval expeditions of Zheng He (Cheng Ho; 1371–1433), who most reputable scholars are convinced did not discover America (as the title of a 2003 best-seller claimed) but did guide a fleet that probably made it as far as Africa.[6]

Other rulers were suspicious of outsiders and took a more restrictive stance toward international connections. They were convinced that increased contact with foreigners was unnecessary and even dangerous.

Most notably, in the late 1700s, the Qing decided to limit Western traders' and missionaries' access to China. Chinese trade with Southeast Asia was robust and operated through many ports, but Westerners eager to exploit new markets for their goods and find new souls to convert were allowed to drop anchor at only one southern city, Guangzhou (Canton). The sole exception to this rule concerned the Portuguese, who had a beachhead of their own in Macao, an island-city near Guangzhou that had been ceded to them as a colony.

What was the Opium War?

The policy of prohibiting foreign ships from anchoring in most Chinese ports was a source of discontent for Westerners who dreamed, as their counterparts of both earlier and more recent times have, of finding in China's heartland an endless supply of customers and converts. They did not believe the Qing line that China was a self-sufficient empire capable of producing all that its people required and that, hence, the West had nothing of great value to offer.

The frustration of Western traders and missionaries grew in the early 1800s as the British desire for (and indeed dependence on) tea produced in China grew. Since European and American merchants had failed to find any product that the Chinese wanted to buy in comparably significant quantities, a trade imbalance favoring China developed, leading to the flow of silver out of the West and into the Qing Empire.

To counteract this, and to take advantage of easy access to the high-quality poppies grown in India, which had become a British colony, traders from Britain began to market opium in China (with US merchants, who often got their poppies from Turkey, following suit). These traders hoped that opium would prove as addictive for the Chinese as tea had proven for Londoners.

The Qing introduced strict laws against buying and selling opium, but the foreign strategy proved effective, and a trade imbalance favoring the West developed. Western traders were always finding new ways to get the drug into China (thanks to help from Chinese smugglers, in many cases), and demand for the narcotic in China consistently grew, particularly in areas near Guangzhou.

Tensions mounted, with each side claiming the moral high ground. The Westerners insisted that free trade was a God-given right that the Qing were barbarically denying them. Western merchants also argued that if only they were granted free access to all Chinese ports, they would find markets for goods other than opium. Qing officials, meanwhile, decried the

Westerners for the villainy of flouting local laws and bringing a dangerous substance into the country.

War broke out in 1839, and Qing forces quickly suffered a series of military defeats. In order to stop Western warships from heading toward the Chinese capital, the Qing signed a treaty very favorable to the foreigners.

What impact did the Opium War have?

The war had devastating effects: economically, it had been costly; politically, it raised doubts among some as to whether the dynasty had a firm hold on the Mandate of Heaven; and, psychologically, the war undermined the longstanding notion among its inhabitants that China was the most advanced and powerful country in the world.[7]

As part of the Treaty of Nanjing signed at the conclusion of hostilities, Britain gained partial control over Hong Kong, which it held as a Crown colony (and, later, a British-dependent territory) until returning it to China in 1997. (Full British control over Hong Kong was accomplished in stages throughout the nineteenth century, concluding in 1898.) Britain also secured the right for its merchants and missionaries to set up self-governing settlements in several other coastal cities, dubbed treaty ports, including Shanghai. The French and Americans soon moved in to establish their own treaty ports, and by the turn of the twentieth century, the Germans, Russians, and Japanese would seek their own concessions.

Why did the Qing Dynasty fall?

Until the 1970s, scholars often viewed the Qing as having had a firm hold on the country up to the Opium War. They presented the story of the first two centuries of Qing rule as one characterized largely by triumphs, with strong and long-reigning emperors extending the reach of the empire into Central Asia. In this narrative, the mid-nineteenth-century clashes with the West marked the beginning of the end of a dynasty that had been thriving. More recently, historians have begun to appreciate that internal matters also strained Qing rule.

What internal developments weakened the Qing?

One source of strain on the Qing was demographic: the population of China grew tremendously in the late 1700s and early to mid-1800s, at least doubling (perhaps tripling or quadrupling) in a century. This placed a great deal of pressure on the country simply because there were more mouths to feed.

The population increase also caused problems for the Qing because the number of local magistrates—fixed at one per county—did not increase. By 1830, each of these multitasking bureaucrats (responsible for presiding over trials, collecting taxes, maintaining granaries, and officiating at local rituals) was overseeing many more people than ever before.

What was the significance of peasant rebellions?

The Qing also faced popular rebellions. These took many forms, ranging from piracy and banditry to religiously inflected insurrections led by self-proclaimed prophets who called on the faithful to rise up. Notable revolts included one led by the Eight Trigrams sect (Bagua jiao) in 1813, which was quickly suppressed, but at the cost of some seventy thousand lives. Another was a holy war launched in the 1820s and 1830s by the Central Asian leader Jahangir Khoja, who sought to free Xinjiang from imperial control.[8]

The White Lotus Rebellion that convulsed much of the Chinese heartland from 1796 until 1804 was even more significant. This revolt was linked to Maitreyan Buddhism, a form of the originally Indian religion that was particularly popular in parts of China and Southeast Asia. The White Lotus Rebellion had a millenarian aspect to it; that is, its followers believed that a new age was about to begin and that those adhering to the faith would fare well in the coming order. Leaders of Chinese Buddhist sects often discouraged outright rebellion, encouraging their followers to wait quietly for change to come. But at some points they called for direct action, and these calls found especially receptive ears among people struggling with natural disasters such as droughts and floods or angered by what they viewed as excessive taxation.[9]

The White Lotus Rebellion, which began with tax protests in a poor mountainous area, was a classic example of a call for action that resonated within an economically desperate population. A potent addition to the mix was anti-Manchu sentiment and Han chauvinism—a conviction that control of China should be returned to members of the main Chinese ethnic group. For some participants, a key attraction of the movement was the belief that it would lead to the restoration of the Ming, the ethnically Chinese dynasty that had preceded the Qing.

The dynasty suppressed the rebellion, but at a great cost. According to a leading historian of Chinese religious movements, the Qing spent "the rough equivalent of five years' revenue (200 million ounces of silver)" on military campaigns against the rebels, and their troops were defeated in enough battles that the "Manchu banner forces' reputation for invincibility" was permanently lost.[10] When the Opium War broke out in 1839, the Qing Dynasty was already reeling from a series of major challenges, contending with both novel issues and popular rebellions of the sort that had toppled previous dynasties.

What was the Taiping Uprising?

The Taiping Uprising (1848–1864) was a millenarian insurrection of enormous proportions, which convulsed the Qing Empire much the way that the roughly contemporaneous Civil War did the United States. The most important nineteenth-century event whose name is still not a household word in the West, its death toll—between twenty and thirty million people—was exponentially higher than its American counterpart.[11]

The leader of this movement, which was just one of the several upheavals that challenged Qing rule during the middle decades of the nineteenth century, was Hong Xiuquan (Hung Hsiu-ch'üan; 1814–1864). A frustrated scholar, his repeated failures to pass the civil-service exams led to a mental breakdown. During this time Hong suffered hallucinations, possibly informed by things he had read in a missionary tract years before, which imbued him with a sense of divine purpose. His visions convinced Hong that he was Christ's younger brother and was destined to expel the Manchus (whom he came to think of as demonic figures and decried as members of a bestial race) from China and transform it into a Christian land. Hong began proselytizing and quickly amassed about ten thousand followers in southern China. His particular version of Christianity was so outlandish to most foreigners that, while he initially gained some Western support, international forces ended up siding with the Qing against him.

By 1850, Hong had begun leading his followers on a military campaign to take over China. Within three years he had established the Taiping Tianguo, or "Heavenly Kingdom of Great Peace," based in the former imperial capital of Nanjing and functioning as a separate state within the Qing realm. At the height of the military struggle, the fiercely anti-Confucian Hong (after failing the exams, he had no fondness for the sage) governed a territory roughly the size of France. He behaved in many ways like the founder of a new dynasty, even instituting a civil-service examination system—with the novel twist that candidates had to demonstrate mastery over his idiosyncratic interpretation of biblical teachings rather than Confucian classics and famous commentaries on those classics, the main staple of Qing official exams.

After settling down in Nanjing, however, Hong and other Taiping leaders began to fight among themselves and the movement faltered. The Taiping government abandoned most of the radical utopian ideals Hong had previously espoused, which included communal ownership of property and complete gender equality. The situation shifted decisively in Qing favor after 1861, when British mercenary soldiers joined the imperial army and began to retake territory from the weakened Taiping. Hong Xiuquan died in 1864, the Heavenly Kingdom he had founded coming to an end shortly thereafter.

Why was the 1894–1895 Sino-Japanese War so important?

The Qing fought further wars with European powers after 1842, including one that ended in 1860 with foreign troops destroying one of the dynasty's most elaborate palaces, Yuanmingyuan. The most significant international conflict of the second half of the nineteenth century, however, was a war with Japan over which country would control the Korean peninsula. The war began in 1894 and concluded a year later with another defeat for the Qing. The Opium War had undermined the notion that the Qing governed the world's most powerful empire; this latest war demonstrated that it was no longer even the dominant regional power in East Asia.

This defeat led some intellectuals to call for the dynasty to embrace the kind of widespread adaptation of Western ideas and institutions that were credited with strengthening Japan, and they gained the ear of a reform-minded emperor. The result was a bold but short-lived effort to radically reshape China's political and educational institutions, which was known as the Hundred Days' Reform of 1898. Conservatives within the dynasty fought back, however, arguing that the West and Japan might have superior armed forces but that Chinese institutions were better, since they were rooted in superior values. This conservative faction won out, and the emperor was placed under house arrest. Despite the short-lived nature of the reforms, some institutions established during this period proved enduring, such as Peking University, which remains China's most prestigious college.

What was the Boxer Rebellion?

The Boxer Rebellion (1899–1901) is greatly misunderstood out-side of China. It began with bands of young men attacking Chinese Christians and foreign missionaries in North China. It took on new dimensions in the summer of 1900, when these insurgents held Western and Japanese residents of Beijing hostage for fifty-five days, and the Qing Dynasty, which had vacillated between viewing the insurgents as bandits to be suppressed and loyalists to be praised, threw their support be-hind the Boxers. An international force of soldiers marching under eight flags (Great Britain, the United States, France, Germany, Italy, Austria-Hungary, Russia, and Japan—the Eight Allied Armies) lifted the siege.

The crisis continued well into 1901, as foreign soldiers carried out campaigns of retribution and members of the Qing ruling family fled the capital. It ended in September 1901, when the Qing Dynasty, which had been allowed to return to Beijing after a brief period of exile in the north, signed a treaty, known as the Boxer Protocol. This accord included a stipula-tion that a giant indemnity be paid to compensate for the loss of foreign lives and property, with no comparable recompense for Chinese suffering at the hands of invading armies.

Another key part of the protocol was designed to justify the continuation of Qing rule. The foreign powers had decided that, for all their complaints about the Qing, they preferred the dynastic devil they knew to any alternative. As a result, as part of the settlement of the crisis, both sides agreed to promote the fiction that the Boxers had been anti-dynastic rebels, rather than members of a loyalist insurrection that had at times re-ceived official support.

How has this crisis been misunderstood?

Western misunderstandings of the Boxer Rebellion begin with the use of misleading nomenclature. It was not really a rebel-lion, for the insurgents often expressed support for the Qing.

The motivation for the uprising was not anger at the dynasty but a desire to rid China of Christianity, which the Boxers blamed for all the ills that had recently befallen the country, including a drought that was causing widespread misery. Another frequent source of misunderstanding is the notion that most of the people the Boxers killed were foreigners, when the vast majority of victims were Chinese Christians.

In addition, the participants did not rely on boxing. The term Boxer was coined by the English-language press because the groups involved made use of martial-arts fighting techniques, claiming that by employing the right mix of drills and rituals they could make themselves impervious to bullets and defeat the better-armed Western forces. At the height of the crisis, however, the Boxer forces sometimes used weapons, and artistic renderings from the time show pitched battles between two armies.

How does the reputation of the crisis differ in China?

In the West and in Japan, the Boxer Rebellion is presented as a tale of the rise and fall of a violent Chinese group. Popular histories linger on discussions of the Boxers' superstitious beliefs, including their notion that they could make themselves impervious to bullets and that railway tracks should be torn up to appease local gods.

In China, by contrast, while the violence and superstitions of the Boxers are sometimes criticized, historians and the Party-state place more emphasis on other aspects of the crisis, such as the grievances that led to the insurrection. These injustices included foreign powers' extending of their reach into Chinese territory over many decades, and the atrocities committed during the "Invasion of the Eight Allied Armies," including the looting of Chinese national treasures and the revenge killing of thousands of northern Chinese. In present-day Chinese accounts, the Boxer Protocol is described as one of many humiliating and unjustly one-sided treaties that foreign powers forced the Chinese to sign.

Why does this difference in views of the Boxers matter?

The Boxer crisis has cast a long shadow over Chinese interactions with foreign countries. Allusions to the events of 1900 have been common whenever conflicts between China and other nations have occurred. Because of how differently the Boxers are viewed, these veer off in opposite directions.

A case in point occurred in May 1999, when NATO bombs hit the Chinese embassy in Belgrade, killing three citizens of the PRC. When Chinese protesters held rowdy demonstrations, hurling objects at the British and US embassies in Beijing and claiming that NATO had intentionally targeted the Chinese embassy in Belgrade, this was decried in some Western media as xenophobic Boxerism. China was once again behaving irrationally, these reports claimed, since the destruction of the Chinese embassy had been an accident.

Some Chinese, however, invoked memories of 1900 in a completely different manner. The events in Belgrade, they insisted, showed that, once again, Westerners were determined to push China around. The fact that NATO includes some of the same powers (e.g., Britain, the United States, and France) that were part of the coalition of Eight Allied Armies that occupied China in 1900 and 1901 gave added force to this very different interpretation of the era of the Boxers.

How did Qing rule finally end?

The Qing Dynasty engaged in a last-ditch effort at radical reform after the Boxer crisis that struck many as too little too late. It was toppled in 1911 by the Xinhai Revolution (Xinhai geming), a series of loosely connected uprisings and mutinies by imperial troops. These led to the abdication of the last emperor and the establishment of a new Republic of China (ROC), which persists, albeit in a greatly reduced territorial form, on Taiwan. The first president of this country was Sun Yat-sen (1866–1925), who was inaugurated on January 1, 1912.

Sun's installation as China's first president was modeled on that of a Western political leader, and efforts were made to convince foreign powers that everything associated with the dynastic system would be abolished. Yet Sun also participated in rituals that harked back to dynastic transitions and played to the anti-Manchu Han nationalism that had been a part of challenges to the Qing since at least the time of the White Lotus Rebellion. He visited the graves of the Ming emperors, for example, in a move that cast the revolution less as a step forward into uncharted terrain than as an act of revenge for the conquest of the country by foreign invaders from the north.[12]

Is imperial China still present in PRC political culture?

In 1992, a prominent American journalist titled his best-selling study of the PRC's first decades *The New Emperors: China in the Era of Mao and Deng*, suggesting that the 1949 revolution that had established the PRC, like the 1911 one that had created the ROC, could be seen as yet another playing out of the dynastic cycle.[13] Other Western writers have used imperial metaphors to underline the way that Mao, like emperors of the past, was a political figure who was also viewed as godlike. Such comparisons also emphasize the secrecy with which the CCP leadership shrouds its operations, and indeed its daily life—sequestered in a heavily guarded compound known as Zhongnanhai, which is located beside the Forbidden City.

In addition, within China there are critics of Communist leaders who employ comparable imagery to discredit figures who claim to represent a revolution that broke completely with the past. For example, during the Tiananmen protests of 1989 (about which more later), demonstrators often described Deng as acting like a dynastic figure. One wall poster, for example, portrayed him as a modern-day counterpart of the Empress Dowager Cixi (Tz'u Hsi; 1835–1908), the mother of one Qing emperor and aunt of another, who functioned as de facto ruler of China for much of her lifetime. (This comparison derived some of its power from the fact that Deng, though China's paramount leader in 1989, did not hold a high formal title, such as party general secretary, president, or prime minister.) In addition, the derisive term princelings (*taizi dang*) is often used to refer to the sons of high-ranking CCP leaders, whom many Chinese view as enjoying unfair advantages and living privileged lives. Perhaps the most infamous princeling is Bo Xilai, a charismatic politician and son of a famous general of Mao's generation who attracted significant popular support as the party secretary of Chongqing municipality before being purged in early 2012 amid a murder scandal and allegations of massive corruption (about which more below).[14]

Xi Jinping, who is both head of the CCP and president of the country, grew up as a princeling, for his father was a onetime comrade of Mao's. He has sought to centralize power in himself to a greater extent than Hu Jintao or other previous leaders did, in a way that some consider imperial. Xi's call for "the great rejuvenation of the Chinese nation" also harks back to the dynastic past, to a time before the Opium War, when China was allegedly strong and able to resist the advances of foreign powers. In 2013, after Xi debuted this slogan, the *Economist* depicted him dressed as the Qianlong Emperor—who ruled the Qing at the apogee of its prosperity and strength—on its cover.[15] Some critics of Xi have pointed out that, at least during its early stages, his campaign to rid the CCP of corrupt officials (about which more below) left untouched those linked by blood to a small coterie of men once in Mao's circle, who constituted a group similar to the family members of dynastic founders.

Invoking imperial imagery to explain or challenge contemporary policies and actions has its value, for it underscores the fact that China is currently beset by some familiar political problems, including high-level corruption rooted in personal access to and sometimes a direct familial relationship with those in high positions. It should not, however, be pushed too far or taken too seriously. In contrast to the ROC, where Chiang Kai-shek was succeeded by his son as president of Taiwan, or for that matter the United States, where two members of the Bush family held the same top post in fairly rapid succession, no two top PRC leaders have been related to one another by blood. And there has always, at least since Mao's time, been an oligarchic aspect to the way the CCP rules, with a group of top leaders, none of whom is kin to another, sharing power in a manner that differs greatly from that of any dynasty. As one Chinese politics specialist has observed, Xi Jinping might be thought of less as a new emperor and more as a CEO.[16]

Moreover, imperial imagery obscures the many ways that the China of today differs from the China of the past. The PRC is changing so quickly that frameworks that suggest it is only able to replicate historical patterns generally distort more than clarify.

And yet, the dynastic cycle and the Mandate of Heaven remain concepts worth keeping in mind. For as we will see in later sections, some of the things that the leaders of the CCP worry about—from the rumblings of popular religious sects to how natural catastrophes are perceived—resemble those that caused emperors to worry about how long their own mandate would last.

3

REVOLUTIONS
AND REVOLUTIONARIES

Who was Sun Yat-sen?

Sun Yat-sen has been hailed as the founding father of the ROC and likened to George Washington in more than a few Chinese textbooks. Sun has the rare distinction of having been treated as a hero on both sides of the Taiwan straits. In the PRC, streets are named after him and on special occasions his portrait is placed in a prominent spot near Tiananmen Square. In the ROC, at least before the Nationalists were first forced to share power with other parties around the turn of the millennium, his image was a central feature of all major political rituals. This special status is made possible by Sun's association with the overthrow of the Qing, and by the fact that he not only founded the Nationalist Party but also brokered the First United Front (1923–1927), an alliance between the Nationalists and the Communists.

Sun's status in revolutionary history is unique, for those the Communists hail as heroes are usually considered villains on Taiwan and vice versa. Unique, too, was the eclectic ideology he espoused, which combined intense nationalism with a cosmopolitan openness to what foreign creeds had to offer.[1]

In his youth, Sun studied medicine in Hong Kong, traveled widely, and developed reform proposals that he tried, unsuccessfully, to bring to the attention of progressive-minded

Qing officials. His transition from reformer to revolutionary occurred in the 1890s, when he began to work with secret societies and to plan anti-Qing uprisings. In 1905, while in Japan, he founded the Revolutionary Alliance, an organization that would eventually evolve into the Nationalist Party.

Even though Sun was subsequently credited with leading the 1911 Revolution, the mutinies and insurrections of October of that year occurred while he was in the United States raising funds for his political ventures. Still, groups with which Sun was affiliated participated in the upheavals, and he soon returned to China to play a key role in the transition to republican rule.

What happened to Sun after he became president?

Sun's presidency was short-lived. Within a year, Yuan Shikai (Yüan Shih-k'ai; 1859–1916) had nudged him out of office. Yuan was a former Qing official and general who had shifted his allegiance to the revolution in 1911 and then in 1912 insisted that he would continue to support the new order only if he were made its president. Lacking an army of his own, Sun felt he had to step aside, though he immediately set about trying to develop a power base from which to reclaim leadership of the country.

Sun never managed to regain control of China, which was run by a succession of military strongmen (often called warlords) until his death in 1925. But the Nationalist Party he founded would, under his successor, Chiang Kai-shek, end up governing China for more than two decades and Taiwan for another half-century.

What was the Warlord Era?

Yuan's assumption of power ushered in a decade-and-a-half-long period during which one or another military strongman was officially designated as China's president. Yet in reality they shared control of the country with a number of powerful regional leaders.

Each of these men had an army and, by virtue of this, effectively controlled a part of the country. Some of these warlords, including Yuan, dreamed of becoming emperors and establishing new dynasties. And even though none of these efforts to formally restore the imperial system proved successful, in political terms the period was a bit of a throwback to the final years of Qing rule, save for the overlay of some of the trappings of a republic, such as, for example, the titles held by officials.[2]

What was the May 4th Movement?

The warlords' abandonment of the revolutionary legacy of 1911 did not go unchallenged. In the years after he was shunted aside, Sun Yat-sen set up operations in the southern city of Guangzhou (Canton), at the head of a revamped Revolutionary Alliance, now rechristened the Nationalist Party. As he dreamed of regaining control of the country, intellectuals agitated for an end to warlord rule and looked to Japan, Russia, and the West for ideas and strategies that could be brought to China to help get the revolutionary project back on track.

Radical teachers and students in Beijing and Shanghai were particularly active in both intellectual exploration—such as translating theoretical and literary works into Chinese and experimenting with new forms of writing—and political mobilization. Their most important collective actions involved protesting the willingness of the warlords to capitulate to demands that foreign powers (especially Japan) made to extend their territorial and economic reach within China. These students and young professors spearheaded an anti-warlord and anti-imperialist drive known as the May 4th Movement.

This political struggle, which was linked to the anti-Confucian New Culture movement discussed in chapter 1, was one of the events that truly changed China. Named for the date in 1919 when a rowdy protest was held in what would later become Tiananmen Square, the specific trigger for it was the way that other countries treated China during the Paris Peace Conference after World War I.

The Allies had claimed that one outcome of the war would be that all nations would have the right to determine their own fates, and that with the defeat of Germany the age of empires would come to an end. Since China had joined, albeit belatedly, the Allies, there seemed good reason to hope that parts of China formerly under German control would return to Beijing's rule. Instead, however, the conference planned to cede these territories on the Shandong Peninsula to Japan in the Treaty of Versailles—and, much to the anger of Chinese students, the warlord government seemed unwilling to fight or even challenge this decision.

On May 4, 1919, students rampaged through Beijing calling for Shandong's return to Chinese control and the dismissal from office of three officials viewed as corrupt and pro-Japanese. After destroying the house of one of these officials, some of these students were arrested and beaten up, one later dying from his wounds. Due in part to the traditional high regard in which scholars were held, members of all urban social classes joined the protests.

The May 4th Movement soon spread to the country's other major cities, with protests in places such as Tianjin, Nanjing, and Guangzhou. The movement reached its peak in early June with a general strike that paralyzed Shanghai, China's main financial and commercial center.

In the end, the Treaty of Versailles took effect unaltered. But the students arrested in the original May 4 protest were all released, the three hated officials were dismissed from office, and the Chinese delegation to the Paris Peace Conference refused to sign the Paris accord. These achievements help explain why later generations would often invoke the May 4th legacy as symbolizing the potential of patriotic mass action.[3]

Who was the most important writer of the May 4th era?

Many authors contributed to the intellectual ferment of the time, but the one whose legacy is richest and most significant is Lu Xun. He is also, arguably, the most significant modern Chinese author whose works remain little known in the West—although his short stories have been translated several times, including in a lively recent translation issued as part of the Penguin Classics series.[4]

Lu Xun's stature is due partly to the range and power of his writings. He was a highly accomplished essayist and author of major short stories, such as the searing anti-Confucian parable "Diary of a Madman," which portrays traditional Chinese values as soul-destroying, and a novella, "The Real Story of Ah Q," which satirizes the 1911 Revolution as a struggle that claimed it could change everything, yet often seemed to do little besides alter the names of the posts held by local officials who bullied the people. He also permanently altered the Chinese political vocabulary, infusing it with terms such as "Ah Qism," referring to the tendency of the eponymous antihero of Lu Xun's novella to change failures into victories when retelling the tales of his exploits.

Lu Xun's works inform Chinese political debates. Though he has been compared to many other Western authors over the years, from the Russian writer Nikolai Gogol (who inspired him) to Nietzsche (one study dubs him China's Gentle Nietzsche), he is perhaps China's closest counterpart to George Orwell. Just as those unfamiliar with Orwell might be confused by English editorials that include casual references to "Big Brother," "Newspeak," and other terms from *1984*, not knowing who Ah Q was or what the implications of describing traditional values as "cannibalistic" are means missing some key subtleties in Chinese political debates.

A final reason for Lu Xun's endurance is that, though for most of his life he was fiercely independent of dogmatisms of the right and the left, he leaned toward the CCP in the years immediately before his death, though he never actually joined the organization. This allowed Mao to elevate him to the status of a revolutionary saint within the PRC. But, as Mao himself once admitted, had Lu Xun lived past 1949 he would likely have ended up running afoul of the new regime. By dying early, however, the way was cleared for the CCP to use him. Between the 1950s and 1970s, his stories were virtually the only contemporary Chinese works of fiction that could be published and read freely.[5]

Here, again, a parallel with Orwell is noteworthy. Orwell, in life, was caustic about the hypocritical aspects of all isms, yet after his death in 1950 he was often made a poster boy for the anti-communist Cold War right.

How does the CCP view the May 4th era?

Lu Xun is by no means the only figure from the May 4th period celebrated in the PRC, for many future leaders of the Communist Revolution, including Mao, were linked to the struggle of 1919. In fact, once in power, the CCP turned the anniversary of the 1919 protests into a national holiday, both to honor youthful patriotism and because the Party views the movement as paving the way for the CCP.

It is certainly true that the popular ferment of 1919, which inspired many youths to think that collective action could help get the revolution back on course, was crucial to the establishment of the CCP. So, too, was the outbreak of the Russian Revolution in 1917, which the New Culture movement journal New Youth hailed as being of epochal importance. The Russian Revolution also turned the attention of many Chinese revolutionaries to Marxism, after a period when radicals had been more drawn to anarchist ideas.

The Russian Revolution was crucial to Chinese activists, not just because of the appeal of its ideals of social equality but because it occurred in a country that was a late-comer to industrialization and seen as backward. Members of the May 4th generation were not only critical of Confucian hierarchies but eager for their country to regain its former stature as a great power. Russia seemed to have found a recipe to both help remake a country domestically and increase its international prestige.[6]

There is debate now over whether the CCP was born in 1920—when important meetings of some future leaders of the organization occurred—or 1921, the date the PRC officially treats as the year of the party's birth. In either version of the story, the central players in its early life included radical Beijing scholars, such as *New Youth* founders Li Dazhao (Li Ta-chao; 1888–1927), the author of an influential essay hailing the "Victory of Bolshevism" in Russia, and Chen Duxiu (Ch'en Tu-hsiu; 1879–1942), a mentor to Mao who advised the students involved in the 1919 demonstrations. Other early members of the CCP besides Mao who were involved in the May 4th protests included Zhou Enlai (Chou En-lai; 1898–1976) and his wife Deng Yingchao (Teng Ying-ch'ao; 1904–1992), who was less known than her husband internationally but was for decades an influential figure in the PRC.

What was the First United Front?

The CCP did not have much of an impact on Chinese politics during its first years in existence. This changed in 1923, when Sun Yat-sen, who was attracted by Moscow's criticism of Western imperialism and the emphasis Lenin had put on the role that a tightly disciplined vanguard party could play in moving a country forward, invited the CCP to join the Nationalists in a united front that would try to both unseat the warlords and fight foreign encroachments. Members of the fledgling CCP accepted the invitation readily; some, including a young Mao, would even hold positions in both parties for a time.

The first significant result of this partnership was the 1925 May 30th Movement, which many saw as picking up where the May 4th Movement had left off. It began when the police in Shanghai's main foreign-run enclave fired into a crowd of protesters who were demonstrating against the mistreatment of Chinese workers in Japanese mills located in the city.

Why was the May 30th Movement significant?

This anti-imperialist struggle, like its 1919 predecessor, spread from being a single-city protest to a national one and culminated in a general strike that paralyzed Shanghai. It did not achieve as many of its stated goals as the May 4th Movement—the unmet demands of May 30th protesters included that Chinese workers at foreign factories be given the right to form unions and that all foreign-run sections of treaty ports be returned to Chinese control. Nevertheless, the propaganda and mobilization work done by activists brought many new converts into both the Nationalist and Communist organizations. This made the latter a political force to be reckoned with,[7] a development paving the way for the end of warlord rule in the wake of the Northern Expedition.

What was the Northern Expedition?

In 1926, Chiang Kai-shek led a joint army of Nationalists and Communists northward from Sun's southern power base in Guangdong (Kwangtung) Province, taking key urban centers as the forces headed toward Beijing. The primary objectives of the expedition were to unseat regional militarists located throughout the country and to unify the nation.

In 1927 the Chinese-run sections of Shanghai (as with other treaty ports, only some parts of the city were under foreign control) fell to the Northern Expedition's troops, thanks to a series of worker uprisings led by the CCP, which prepared the groundwork for the arrival of Chiang Kai-shek's soldiers.

Later that same year, Chiang, who had succeeded Sun as head of the Nationalists following the latter's death in March

1925, took the nearby city of Nanjing (literally, "southern capital" due to its occasional status as the country's political center during imperial times). Chiang established the Republic's central government in Nanjing. Then, in 1928, Chiang's forces took Beijing (whose name means "northern capital") and renamed it Beiping ("northern peace") to show that the political center remained in the south.[8]

Who was Chiang Kai-shek?

Chiang was often called simply "Generalissimo," because of his role as leader of the Northern Expedition forces and his military background and bearing. An enigmatic figure, before committing himself to the revolution against the warlords he had joined a secret society, established ties with the Green Gang (a powerful organized-crime syndicate based in Shanghai), and received military training in Japan.

He developed close personal ties to Sun Yat-sen via common revolutionary activities. These took on an added dimension when Chiang married Song Meiling (Soong May-ling; 1897–2003). A US-educated Christian, Song Meiling was the sister of Sun's widow, Song Qingling (Soong Ch'ing-ling; 1893–1981), who never formally joined the CCP but remained on the mainland after 1949, when the PRC was founded, and served as an official.

Aside from his skills as a military strategist, the Generalissimo proved very effective at forming alliances that helped him navigate the factional politics of the Nationalist Party. These were complex because several people, most notably Sun's close confidante Wang Jingwei (Wang Ching-wei; 1883–1944), thought that *they* should succeed Sun as leader of the organization.[9]

Whether he ever shared Sun's conviction that the cause of the Chinese revolution was best served by an alliance with the Communists is unclear, but by late 1926 Chiang felt that the First United Front was a mistake. In April 1927, with help from the Green Gang, he carried out the White Terror, a vicious purge of CCP members in Shanghai. Chiang's allies imprisoned and killed some of the very people who had helped deliver the Chinese-run parts of the city to the Northern Expedition forces.

From that point on until his death in 1975, Chiang treated the Communists as a great threat to China's future. In the face of the Japanese encroachment into Chinese territory that preceded the outbreak of World War II, he was forced to ally with the Communists again during the Second United Front (1937–1945). He was pressured into this pragmatic arrangement after being taken hostage in Xi'an in 1936 by a warlord who thought China's only hope for salvation lay in unity between warring factions. But Chiang's anti-communism was deeply felt and enduring, and he continued to argue that, as he put it, the Japanese were only a "disease of the skin," while the Communists were a "disease of the heart"—that is, ultimately the graver threat to Chinese national survival.

What was the Long March?

Chiang Kai-shek's White Terror purges almost succeeded in eliminating the CCP in 1927. The Communists, however, proved impossible to eradicate completely.

Some members of the organization avoided detection and operated underground cells within cities held by the Nationalists, while others escaped to rural base areas. In the early 1930s, Chiang tried several times to encircle those base areas and destroy the main clusters of remaining Communists. To escape this fate, the CCP abandoned its temporary headquarters in the southern province of Jiangxi in 1934 and began a torturous trek northward that became known as the Long March.

This journey ended in 1935 with the Communists setting up new base areas in Shaanxi Province, the most famous in Yan'an. Here the Communists began to experiment with bold policies, such as land-redistribution campaigns, that eventually won them support from many poor Chinese and also impressed some Western visitors (most famously the US journalist Edgar Snow).[10]

In official PRC histories, the Long March is treated as an event of mythic significance and proportions, and it is easy to see why. The odds against a straggling band of guerrillas escaping the better-armed Nationalist forces while traveling thousands of miles to safety over often-treacherous terrain are staggering: eighty-six thousand people traversed six thousand miles in just over a year, crossing eighteen mountain ranges and twenty-four rivers. But only some eight thousand of those who began the trip completed it; the remainder fell victim to illness and exhaustion, died in military clashes with the Nationalists, or deserted.[11]

Had the Long March failed, the CCP would have ceased to play a role in Chinese politics and history, but the march had another significant outcome: it was during this epic exodus that Mao consolidated his position as supreme leader of the party. He could do this in part because other CCP leaders endorsed his vision of guerrilla warfare as the strategy to use in fighting the Nationalists. Though he would turn against some of his comrades-in-arms from the Long March in the "rectification campaigns" (in effect, purges) of the early-to-mid-1940s and break with others after the founding of the PRC, Mao's closest allies from the 1930s on tended to be fellow Long March veterans. If a Communist leader had spent the 1930s and 1940s doing underground work in a White city controlled by the Nationalists rather than in a Red area like Yan'an—and hence been further from Mao's direct influence and closer to the temptations of a mode of life he viewed as bourgeois and decadent—they were vulnerable after 1949 to charges of political impurity. In particular, they were more likely to be dubbed capitalist roaders, beaten up by Red Guards loyal to Mao, subjected to public criticism, and even tortured during the Cultural Revolution—about which more below.[12]

What was the Rape of Nanjing?

The period of Japanese occupation, which began with Japan taking over parts of Manchuria in 1931, remains a topic of bitter memory in China. A particularly significant event in this regard was the so-called Rape of Nanjing (Nanking), which unfolded in late 1937 and early 1938, when the Japanese Army moved south to attack the capital of the ROC. According to one US survey of Chinese history, during a short horrific period in Nanjing, "an estimated 200,000 to 300,000 Chinese were killed" and "an estimated 20,000 women were raped" by Japanese soldiers.[13]

The Japanese invasion in general (there were atrocities committed in many parts of the country) and the Rape of Nanjing in particular continue to bedevil Sino–Japanese relations. This is in part because some textbooks approved for use in Japan downplay the extent of the atrocities, and some conservative historians deny that they occurred at all. Additionally, Tokyo, though officially expressing regret for the invasions of the 1930s and 1940s, has stopped short of carrying out a thoroughgoing repudiation of all aspects of its World War II behavior, such as that undertaken by Germany.

How did the Communists beat the Nationalists?

Many factors contributed to Mao's defeat of Chiang in 1949. For example, the way that World War II played out fostered an image of the Communists as more devoted patriots than the Nationalists. The Nationalists and the Communists had allied to fight Japan from 1937 on, but many Chinese were left feeling that the latter organization was more wholeheartedly committed to fighting imperialism than was the former, which had trouble shaking its reputation for being corrupt and led by a man obsessed with the idea that communism was as big a threat as foreign invaders.

When the Japanese finally surrendered in August 1945, many hoped a period of peace and stability would begin. This was not to be. The rapprochement between the Nationalists and Communists, which had long been strained, collapsed completely within months. A civil war broke out almost immediately, lasting until 1949, when Mao's Red Army, known as the People's Liberation Army (PLA), took control of several key cities. These included Shanghai and Beiping, whose name the Communists changed back to Beijing, signaling that it was once again China's capital.

Throughout the civil war, pitched battles were fought in the countryside, and more symbolic struggles, via propaganda and demonstrations, were waged in the cities. The Communists promised that if they won they would redistribute land. This pledge gained them support in many villages, especially since word had circulated that land-reform programs (in which landlords were stripped of their holdings and sometimes beaten and even killed) had been occurring for years in areas under CCP control. Meanwhile, disgust with official corruption, Nationalist infighting, government censorship drives, crackdowns on urban demonstrations, and a sense that the Generalissimo was too beholden to the United States alienated many intellectuals in the cities.

The United States backed the Nationalists (with some reservations), while the Soviet Union backed the Communists (likewise with ambivalence), as was expected in those early days of the Cold War. Chiang later insisted that Moscow's support was the key to Mao's victory, but equally or more important was Chiang's failure to run the country effectively in the late 1940s, most evident in inflation of such staggering proportions that city dwellers sometimes needed wheelbarrows-full of nearly worthless currency to buy rice.[14]

Given how much intellectuals distrusted the Nationalists by the late 1940s, the reputation that the Communists had earned among workers and farmers as an organization that championed the interests of the common people, and the desire of Chinese of all classes for a time of peace, it is no wonder that many saw the end of the civil war as a very welcome development. The year 1949 was hailed in the Communist Party press at the time as a moment of "liberation" (*jiefang*), a term that continues to be used to this day in the PRC as shorthand for that year. This is surely what it felt like to many people at that point, though some, such as landlords, were bound to see it as a fearful rather than welcome thing that the CCP had taken control of the country. Others would also soon have misgivings about the turn the nation had taken. But in the early 1950s, with the country at peace and living standards rising, most felt that China was moving in a positive direction.

What role have mass campaigns played in the PRC?

Throughout the first decades of CCP rule in China, mass campaigns orchestrated by the government were an important feature of daily life. These drives, as they might be called, which were used to publicize and ensure compliance with new policies, would remain important during the two years immediately following Mao's death in 1976, when Hua Guofeng held power. After Hua was demoted and Deng Xiaoping took charge in 1978, campaigns became less common, but they have sometimes played a significant role, even in what is known as the Reform Era.

While the content of these campaigns has varied greatly, their formats have been similar. High officials give speeches and leading newspapers publish editorials spelling out the goals of the drive, and city streets are covered with banners containing key slogans, as are public buildings in both urban and rural settings. Party representatives, the heads of neighborhood associations (important grassroots-level authority figures during the early decades of the PRC in particular), and leaders of the individual *danwei* (government work units) all take charge of getting their subordinates to participate in rallies and other activities. And sometimes individuals or activities representing ideas or practices the campaign is meant to counteract are singled out for criticism.

According to a top CCP official, early campaigns were an effort, above all, to ensure that the goals of the Party were internalized, to get the people to "emancipate themselves step by step, instead of [the government] imposing revolution on the masses or bestowing victory on the masses as a favor."[15] Among important early mass campaigns was the Land Reform drive, which extended to new areas the redistribution of landlords' holdings and included verbal and physical assaults on anyone viewed as belonging to the vilified landlord class. This campaign, as noted, had begun in Yan'an and other areas under CCP control before 1949. But the first PRC nationwide movement was the one designed to publicize and gain compliance with the New Marriage Law of 1950 (about which more below).

What was the Resist America, Support Korea campaign?

The goal of the Resist America, Support Korea campaign was to solidify the reputation of the CCP as a patriotic organization determined to ensure that China would never again be pushed around by foreign powers. It began as soon as the Korean War (1950–1953) started.

This first hot war of the Cold War era, which pitted allies of the Soviet Union against allies of the United States, ended in a stalemate, creating the division between communist North Korea and non-communist South Korea that exists to this day. Despite the military impasse, Mao claimed that the war represented a great victory for China. The PRC contributed the largest number of troops to the North Korean cause, and more Chinese died during the struggle than members of any other foreign population, with Mao's own son among the casualties. Propaganda posters, films, and stories celebrated the heroics of Chinese soldiers, while those on the home front attended rallies against American imperialism and donated money to support the war effort. At the same time, the CCP embarked upon an intense effort to root out alleged spies, targeting those with connections to foreign governments, businesses, churches, and schools, as well as Chiang's Nationalists.

The victory, according to Mao, lay in the Communist forces' ability to prevent the Americans and their allies from taking control of the entire Korean peninsula. This proved that China could hold its own against apparently superior powers. Another victory was that enjoyed by the CCP, which had used the campaign to consolidate its control over both businesses and people throughout the country.[16]

What was the Hundred Flowers Campaign?

The Hungarian Uprising of 1956, which was suppressed only with Moscow's help, sent shock waves throughout the communist world. This revolt exposed as a myth the idea that the communist leaderships of all countries linked to the Soviet Union—a category that included China at that point, since aid and advisers from Moscow were playing important roles in the nation—enjoyed broad popular support. It also exposed as illusory the notion that the state socialist lands of Central and Eastern Europe were allies as opposed to merely satellites of the Soviet Union.

The Chinese response to this included Mao's call for a loosening of the taboo on constructive criticism of CCP rule. The slogan used for this 1956 initiative was "Let a Hundred Flowers Bloom and a Hundred Schools of Thought Contend," an allusion to the distant Warring States period, when proponents of Confucian, Daoist, Legalist, and many other visions of morality and statecraft had competed for the attention and patronage of local rulers. Soon professors and students around the country were writing memorials and putting up wall posters calling for change.

Some scholars of the Mao years have interpreted the Hundred Flowers Campaign as a cynical effort by Mao to smoke out all intellectuals with dangerous ideas. A competing interpretation, also widely accepted, holds that it was meant to demonstrate that the CCP was popular enough and firmly enough in control that it could benefit from advice, and by doing this further increase its support among intellectuals. In this view, the crackdown on critics that soon came was a response to the unexpectedly harsh nature of the commentary unleashed.

In either case, the end result was that a brief flourishing of open discussion was followed by a series of purges. These purges were known as the Anti-Rightist Campaign.

What happened during the Anti-Rightist Campaign?

The Anti-Rightist Campaign, which started in 1957, was a drive used to inculcate intellectual orthodoxy. Anyone who expressed or was simply accused of harboring unorthodox views risked being designated a counter-revolutionary and enemy of the people, subjected to public criticism, sent to a prison camp, or all of the above. Once incarcerated, these Rightists would experience a period of either reform through labor or reeducation that, if successful, would allow them to reenter society. They would never be able to fully shake the stigma of having once been labeled a Rightist, since the government kept a file on every citizen of the PRC, which included notes on the individual's political history. This dossier system, which has still not been completely abandoned, meant that nearly all citizens were subjected to the kind of close and enduring scrutiny that members of selectively targeted groups have been in periods of unusually intense US monitoring, such as Red Scares.

In addition to those who actually expressed criticism of the new regime, some people suffered during the Anti-Rightist Campaign for quite different reasons. Some were labeled Rightists because individuals who held grudges against them or wanted to burnish their own reputations for political rectitude concocted tales of the targeted person's failings. Others were singled out purely to fill implicit quotas motivated by

Mao's comments that class enemies constituted a certain percentage of the population.

How did women fare during the first decade of the PRC?

Given the central role of family relations in Confucian thought and the bias against women within late imperial society, it is telling that one of the first pieces of legislation enacted by the CCP government was the New Marriage Law of 1950. The most conservative elements of traditional China's patriarchal culture had been expressed through everything from demands for widows to remain chaste, to girls being pressured to bind their feet (in a painful process that among other things limited their physical mobility), to only men being able to take official examinations. It is true that some noteworthy reforms of gender and family relations were made during the Republican period (1912–1949). Most notably, women were granted the right to vote in 1947—admittedly something of a Pyrrhic victory, given that in the civil war era elections had so little value—and foot-binding (never a universal practice and something that varied widely between regions and across class and ethnic lines) became much less common. But once Chiang Kai-shek took power, the celebration of Confucianism, interpreted in very traditional ways, put a check on greater equality between the sexes.

The Communists thought that introducing a new marriage system, in which family elders were not the key determinants of who would marry whom, and men and women would be treated equally, would change socio-economic relations within villages. It also signaled that a truly new order had begun—that this revolution would lead to much more than simply changing the titles given to local power-holders.[17]

The Marriage Law campaign championed the idea that betrothals should be between freely consenting individuals, rather than arranged by family elders. The law also stipulated that, once married, husbands and wives would be treated the same, with both parties having equal ability to seek divorce (something that under the old system had been much easier for men). Though the New Marriage Law did not officially require this, one symbolically significant shift that accompanied its implementation was the substitution of the CCP for the husband's family in ritual aspects of weddings. This was represented by the fact that in post-1949 marriages, a portrait of Mao often occupied places in the home traditionally reserved for lineage ancestors. Moreover, during the marriage ceremony, couples bowed before Mao's likeness as they had once bowed before the husband's parents.

Mao and the CCP proclaimed that "women hold up half the sky," promising the dawn of a new era in gender relations. In some respects, life for Chinese women did improve during the early years of the PRC. Many assumed positions of responsibility in their local party units, while others found themselves lauded as "model workers" for their labor productivity. A campaign promoting safe childbirth also yielded dramatic improvements in maternal and infant mortality.

Yet there were limits to the revolution in gender relations that Mao and other CCP leaders promised. While many women did join the labor force and began working in offices, factories, or, toward the end of the 1950s, on collective farms, they also remained the primary caregivers for their families, often working a "second shift" to complete their household's cooking, cleaning, washing, sewing, and other tasks associated with childrearing. As a result, many Chinese women might remember the first decade of the PRC as a time of progress, but also as one of exhaustion.[18]

What sort of people were Mao and his main allies?

Mao was born into a middling sort of rural family (his father had enough money to employ a laborer and to educate his sons), but in his youth he gravitated toward radical politics. He did this first within his native Hunan Province and later in Beijing, where he worked as a librarian and was influenced greatly by progressive teachers, especially Chen Duxiu, who had begun to promote anarchist and Marxist ideas. Mao's most significant early writings included a 1927 report on the Hunan Peasant Movement, in which he stressed the CCP's need to learn from the actions of rural activists (rather than assume, in a more orthodox Marxist fashion, that farmers were an inherently backward group who needed guidance from urbanites); claimed that extreme tactics and great violence were often a necessary part of revolutionary settings (this is where his famous statement that "a revolution is not a dinner party" appears); and noted that women were uniquely oppressed in China (not only suffering from class injustices but also having power wielded over them by male relatives).

Mao rose to power within the CCP during the Long March, as already noted, and when the PRC was founded his supremacy was symbolized by the fact that it was he who stood atop Tiananmen (Beijing's Gate of Heavenly Peace) and proclaimed the establishment of the new country. The giant portrait of his face, which still hangs near that spot, is a reminder of his role as the first paramount leader of the PRC. Mao insisted that he did not want to be the subject of a personality cult, and even prohibited celebrations of his birthday, and yet he did many things that contributed to his elevation to a godlike status within the PRC during his lifetime. The official version of CCP history promoted from 1949 until 1976 cast him as the central player in each and every defining moment of the revolution from the early 1920s onward, unfairly downplaying the contributions of many others. And celebrations of holidays such as those marking the anniversaries of the founding of the CCP (July 1), the founding of the Red Army (August 1), and even the founding of the country (October 1) became, in effect, as much celebrations of Mao as the collectivities they ostensibly honored.

Mao's closest associates, as mentioned, were mostly other Long March veterans. These included Zhou Enlai, who was known for his diplomatic skills, and Zhu De (Chu Te; 1886–1976), the second-most-important PLA leader. They were also the people who had worked most closely with Mao in Yan'an, the village where the policies that would guide the early years of the PRC were first developed and tested and which became a pilgrimage site for those who viewed these leaders as sacred figures. A smaller number of early PRC leaders had spent the 1930s and 1940s in Nationalist-controlled urban centers, where they carried out underground propaganda efforts and organized workers. One such individual was Liu Shaoqi (Liu Shao-ch'i; 1898–1969), Mao's heir apparent in the 1950s and early 1960s.

Like Mao, many of his allies had first become politically active during or just before the New Culture movement and had been involved in anti-imperialist and anti-warlord protests of the 1910s. Some had studied abroad in their youths (Zhou spent time in France, as had Deng Xiaoping, also a Long March veteran), while others, including Mao, did not leave the country for the first time until much later in life (in his case not until going to Moscow in 1949)—if they ever left it at all.

How were Mao's writings viewed?

The CCP initially treated Mao's speeches and essays as the most influential domestic interpretations of Marxism. Soon, however, due to Mao's own efforts and those of his closest allies, they began to function as holy scripture: texts that were studied compulsively, memorized, and used as the final arbiters of right and wrong in nearly any dispute or legal matter.

This contributed to and expressed Mao's general elevation to godlike status, which was visually represented in the many statues, giant portraits, and innumerable posters that celebrated his accomplishments and treated him as the embodiment of the revolution and indeed of the New China—a term still used to refer to the nation established in 1949.[19]

His writings covered a wide spectrum of issues, as he crafted theoretical texts that endorsed his modification of Marxism regarding the revolutionary potential of peasants, wrote poems in classical style, and stressed the importance of guerrilla warfare as a method for numerically and militarily weaker groups to attain power. Always a critic of Western imperialism, from the late 1950s on Mao also devoted much of his writing to denouncing the Soviet Union for shifting from revolutionary to revisionist positions. A split between Moscow and Beijing, tied to disputed borders and to different views of the international communist movement, opened up in the early 1960s and lasted for more than two decades. Mao insisted that China's version of communism—not the Soviet Union's—provided the best model for revolutionaries in developing countries to follow because it emphasized the revolutionary potential of the peasantry and stressed anti-imperialist action. It was the only way forward.

What was the Great Leap Forward?

By the late 1950s, Mao had become impatient. He wanted China to move more rapidly toward achieving the egalitarian utopia of true communism—and to show the world that his country was more than just one of many junior partners in the global communist movement led by the Soviet Union.

This prompted him to push for a bold new project, one designed to convince both his followers at home and foreign observers that China was capable of excelling in certain areas. Moreover, Mao wanted to demonstrate that China could even become equal to or surpass the strongest countries of the West. He called for abandoning go-slow policies, based on step-by-step moves toward higher levels of collectivization, and pursuing instead a "Great Leap Forward," which would be achieved through rapid collectivization and ambitious campaigns to increase crop yields and raise steel production, all intended to help China achieve full-blown communism before the Soviet Union and gain economic parity with the West.

The initial results of the program seemed impressive, as CCP cadres and the press reported enormously high crop yields. Reports also filled newspapers of the "happier collective life" that peasants were enjoying as they made the most of the new group "dining rooms, kindergartens, nurseries, sewing groups, barber shops, public baths, happy homes for the aged," and so forth that communes provided.[20] Beneath the surface, however, fault lines were forming. Fearing that the central authorities would punish them for being insufficiently supportive of Mao's directives if they failed to report exciting results, local officials overstated the size of crop yields. Additionally, in order to boost steel-production figures, officials directed rural peasants to melt down useful farm implements, which created not the quality steel desired but useless (except for bragging purposes) hunks of metal. The Great Leap Forward is also known for Mao's endorsement of pseudo-scientific innovations, such as planting crops closer together to boost harvest levels, which were dismal failures.

When these problems were compounded by bad weather, the result was the most lethal famine in world history: lasting until 1961, it claimed somewhere between twenty and thirty million lives. The famine hit the young unusually hard: the median age of those dying in China plunged from a 1957 level of 17.6 years to a 1963 level of 9.7 (i.e., half of the dead that year were under 10 years old). As one historian put it, "the Great Leap Forward, launched in the name of strengthening the nation by summoning all the people's energies, had turned back on itself and ended by devouring its young."[21] It would not be the last moment of self-destructiveness, though the next time it was the old who would be devoured.

What was the Cultural Revolution?

After the Great Leap disaster, several of the highest-ranking party officials pressured Mao to step back from his position as China's paramount leader. Though Mao was still officially venerated as the nation's greatest thinker, Liu Shaoqi, Deng Xiaoping, and other CCP leaders regarded as more pragmatic and less utopian took over the actual running of the country. The Cultural Revolution, which remains one of the least-understood events in modern Chinese history, both inside and outside of China, was largely an effort by Mao to reclaim his central position by going around the party bureaucracy and appealing directly to the masses.

The struggle began with Mao, who worried that the revolution was ossifying, issuing militant statements and then presiding over massive rallies of passionate loyalist youths known as Red Guards in the summer of 1966. The Cultural Revolution period is well known for young people's verbal—and sometimes physical—assaults on anyone they viewed as insufficiently devoted to their hero. In scores if not hundreds or thousands of cases, Red Guards beat to death these so-called enemies of the people, including teachers and school administrators they accused of being too conservative or not respectful enough of Mao's teachings.

The years that followed were marked by back-to-back political campaigns, in which many high-ranking leaders became targets of angry crowds. It was a time of chaotic purges and counter-purges, when the victims of one wave could become the bullies of the next. Liu Shaoqi went from being Mao's chosen successor to the target of a mass campaign, a fate that eventually also befell his replacement, Lin Biao (Lin Piao; 1907–1971). During this period, campuses were closed and urban students sent to rural areas, where they were meant to purify themselves by working the land, in the "Up to the Mountains, Down to the Countryside" campaign.

The Cultural Revolution was a time of street clashes and rural violence, in which many innocent people suffered, whether from having their reputations damaged or being harassed so intensely that they killed themselves. It was a time of utopian hopes turning into dark nightmares, an era when children betrayed their parents and friends betrayed friends, swept up in the ideological fervor of a particular campaign or simply a desire for self-preservation; in this setting the safest thing to do was often to find others to denounce to prove one's own virtue. The campaign had many of the characteristics of a fundamentalist religious movement, with Mao in the role of prophet and his works becoming the gospel. It was also an effort led by youths who had grown up surrounded by films and posters that told them the only way to live a meaningful life was to take part in epic acts of upheaval and to create new equivalents to the Long March and Yan'an period. Red Guards reenacted those earlier times by traveling around China (these journeys were framed as efforts to spread Mao's teachings and share revolutionary experiences with one another), sometimes by train and sometimes on foot (whenever they could, literally walking through terrain that Mao had traversed three or four decades earlier).

What was the Gang of Four?

The Gang of Four refers to a coterie of "leftist" radicals consisting of Mao's third wife, and later widow, Jiang Qing (Chiang Ch'ing; 1914–1991), and three of her allies. Jiang and Mao had been married since the Yan'an years, but until the mid-1960s, thirty years later, she remained mostly absent from elite politics. This changed, though, when she began promoting radical literature and performing arts at the outset of the Cultural Revolution. By its end, she and the others exerted a great deal of power. After Mao's death in 1976, Jiang and the other Gang of Four members themselves were imprisoned and became targets of mass campaigns.

In their 1980 trial, televised nationwide, prosecutors working under the guidance of CCP leadership used the Gang of Four as scapegoats for the mistakes of the Cultural Revolution in a manner that partially mitigated Mao's responsibility for the *luan* (turmoil) of the era.[22] In an outcome that had been certain before the trial even began, the Gang of Four members were all convicted of anti-CCP activities and sentenced to long prison terms. They are presented in official PRC histories as scheming, unprincipled opportunists who took advantage of their connections to Mao to carry out a nefarious plot to destroy the country and assume absolute power. Their method was to label as Rightists anyone they disliked or viewed as a competitor (such as Deng Xiaoping), while embracing an exaggerated form of leftism that claimed to be ultra-revolutionary but that in fact endangered the revolution. Jiang, who committed suicide in prison in 1991, is now mostly remembered in China as a villainous woman whose self-interested schemes could have toppled the state, demonized as a "dragon lady" in the style of imperial wives during China's dynastic past.[23]

Why hasn't Mao been repudiated by China's current leaders?

Varying assessments of Mao have always existed. There are even places outside of China, such as Nepal, where Maoist guerrillas treat his writings as gospel. Still, of late it has become very common outside of China to refer to Mao as a counterpart to Hitler or Stalin, largely because of the damage his policies did to the country during the Great Leap Forward and the Cultural Revolution.

The Hitler analogy is a misleading one in many ways, but it must be understood before its flaws can be explained. This is an important issue to address because if Mao is thought of simply as a Hitler with Chinese characteristics then it is bound to seem bizarre and disturbing, to say the least, that his face appears on PRC banknotes, his body lies preserved in Tiananmen Square, and references to carrying forward "Mao Zedong Thought" still show up in National Day slogans.

Published in 2005, Jung Chang and Jon Halliday's best-selling biography *Mao: The Unknown Story*[24] has become the most famous English-language biography of Mao. It is also the most extreme in its negative view of him. Not content to locate Mao within a triumvirate of evil that includes Hitler and Stalin (as writers before them had done), Chang and Halliday go further, presenting him as in some ways the vilest of the three. The book includes a controversial claim that is now routinely repeated as a simple statement of fact: Mao was responsible for seventy million peacetime deaths, more than any other leader in history.

This figure is based on the argument that Mao killed everyone who died during the Great Leap famine, instead of having implemented misguided policies that precipitated a catastrophic event. Furthermore, in this line of argument every victim of the purges and mass campaigns from the 1950s through the mid-1970s who died in prison or committed suicide, in addition to those slain during the Cultural Revolution clashes, represents a peacetime death to be laid at his door. That number itself is impossible to verify, partly because it is difficult to separate starvation from other causes of death in famine years. It is also impossible to separate mortality resulting from political violence from death caused by old age or illness during times of civil strife.

In addition, a focus solely on catastrophe leaves out of the picture completely the achievements of the first decades of the PRC. The fact remains that, despite all of the horrors of the Great Leap Forward, Mao's time in power saw life expectancy within China double from roughly thirty-five years to seventy, helped in part by a dramatic lowering of infant mortality, while illiteracy declined even more sharply (from approximately 80 to under 10 percent).

Mao: The Unknown Story portrays Mao as a heartless Machiavellian figure, even demonic. He never even truly believed in Marxism, the authors claim, but embraced the creed simply as a way to gain power. Moreover, they assert that, late in life, Mao became a bloodthirsty and sexually depraved tyrant who interacted only with sycophants.

Was Mao a monster?

There are many alternatives to thinking of Mao as China's Hitler and/or Stalin.[25] One is to view him as American scholars view Andrew Jackson, a controversial figure whose face for many decades has appeared on twenty-dollar bills. Jackson is remembered both as having played a significant role in the development of a political organization (the Democratic Party) that still has many partisans, and as responsible for brutal policies toward Native Americans that are now often referred to as genocidal, as well as a defender of slavery (hence the movement to remove his face from banknotes, which seemed to have succeeded but has been called into question by the 2016 election of Donald Trump, who admires Jackson).

Jackson, for all his flaws, has often been invoked, including by Trump, as representing an egalitarian strain within the American democratic tradition, a self-made man of the people who rose to power via straight talk and was not allied with moneyed elitists. Mao, whose face began to appear on Chinese banknotes after his death and still graces them, stands for something roughly similar. Workers in state-owned industries who in recent years have been laid off associate Mao with a time when laborers got more respect, and he is remembered by some as a Communist leader who, for all his mistakes, never forgot his roots in the countryside and never viewed himself as superior to ordinary folk.

What is the current Chinese government's view of Mao?

Contrary to what many in the West believe, the Chinese population has not been brainwashed into thinking that the CCP and its leaders are infallible, and today, very few people in China still revere Mao as a godlike figure. There is a widespread acceptance of the fact that Mao made major mistakes that wreaked havoc on the lives of millions. The official verdict, first put forward in the early 1980s, holds that across his time in power Mao was 70 percent right and 30 percent wrong. Some Chinese think this too harsh a report card for the leader who made China fully independent of foreign powers for the first time in a century; others think it far too generous an assessment of him.

Mao's mistakes are not spelled out in the official account of his legacy. There is a widespread acknowledgement, though, that his biggest missteps came late in life. It is understood that his most egregious errors included the Great Leap and the Cultural Revolution. In respect to the former, Mao is blamed for encouraging pseudo-scientific practices and creating a political environment in which officials felt the need to falsify statistics; with the latter, he is blamed for spurring the Red Guards on to militancy in 1966 and facilitating or at least doing too little to stop the Gang of Four in the 1970s. When people in China revere him now, the Mao they have in mind is often the leader of the Long March and victory over the Nationalists.

How do ordinary Chinese feel about Mao?

The feelings of ordinary Chinese toward Mao run the gamut— from nostalgia to fury, admiration to disdain. There continue to be long lines to view his body, which remains on display in the lavish mausoleum in the center of Tiananmen Square that was built soon after his death. But not everyone who goes to look at him does so in a spirit of reverence (it has long been said that there are those who go just to make sure that the tyrant they feared and hated is really dead), though a small minority pay homage to a man they still think of as a kind of deity. Most have a mindset not unlike that which citizens of today's France might have when visiting Napoleon's tomb, considering Mao a person of undeniable importance in their country's past, who had his dark side but also made significant contributions without which the nation would not be the global power it is now.

Expressing admiration for Mao in contemporary China can serve as a means of criticizing things that have happened since his death. For example, early in the twenty-first century, workers in northern Chinese rust-belt cities—newly laid off from state-run enterprise jobs that Mao had promised would be theirs for life—sometimes carried his portrait during their demonstrations. Mao portraits made another appearance in anti-Japanese protests that took place in the fall of 2012. The presence of the portraits suggested that China once again needed a "Great Helmsman" (as Mao had been known) to stand up to the Japanese and settle a territorial dispute between the two countries, as well as steer China back on course more generally.[26]

Some Chinese who lived through and suffered during the Cultural Revolution refer to specific things about it—and, by extension, Mao—in a positive way. If annoyed with the self-centeredness and materialism of contemporary youths, they may say that as bad as the Cultural Revolution was, having young urbanites experience peasant life firsthand was a good thing.[27]

There are also those who remember Mao in part as the man who achieved important foreign-policy goals, such as helping North Korea battle South Korean and United Nations forces to a draw in the 1950s. Or they might view positively Mao's historic 1972 meeting with Richard Nixon, made possible by the fact that the great Chinese modifier of Marxism and the fervently anti-communist US president shared an antipathy toward and desire to neutralize the Soviet Union. This paved the way for the reestablishment of full diplomatic ties between Beijing and Washington in the late 1970s, when Jimmy Carter was the US president and Deng Xiaoping China's paramount leader.

Sometimes it is even precisely the qualities of Mao that Chang and Halliday cite as proof of his villainy, such as his alleged inability to feel true affection for his own blood relations, that are turned into positive traits. For example, when angered by the power and privilege enjoyed by the princelings of today, some people say that Mao's superiority to his successors is shown by how he treated his progeny. When he sent his son abroad, they note, it was to risk his life alongside his compatriots in war-torn Korea. When Mao's successors send their progeny abroad, it is to Oxford, Cambridge, Stanford, or the Harvard School of Business.

Part II

THE PRESENT
AND THE FUTURE

This half of the book will focus on China today and China tomorrow. It begins with a chapter called "From Mao to Now," which looks at some of the most significant figures (such as Deng Xiaoping), policies (such as the famous if somewhat misleadingly named "One-Child" Policy), and events (including 1989's Tiananmen protests and the 2008 Olympics) of the last four decades. One central topic it explores is the surprising longevity of the CCP, an organization that many felt was on its last legs in 1989 and yet is now preparing to celebrate its hundredth anniversary in 2021. The second chapter in this section is intended to help readers make sense of a time when the United States and China are the world's two leading economic and political powers. It looks at some of the ways that the United States has misunderstood and continues to misunderstand China, often because it fails to appreciate just how diverse the PRC is. After that, the chapter turns the tables to look, more briefly, at Chinese misconceptions about the United States, which often arise from a failure to appreciate how different the US and Chinese media systems are. The section, and the book, ends with some forecasts about the future, and some suggestions about how in the years to come the people of the United States and the people of China might begin to see more clearly the big country across the Pacific from them.

4

FROM MAO TO NOW

Who was Deng Xiaoping?

Deng's first revolutionary experiences were as a student in France in the 1920s, when he developed a lasting friendship with a fellow radical youth named Zhou Enlai (throughout much of the Mao era, the second-most-important person in China) and became known as "Dr. Mimeograph" because of his role in publicizing progressive causes. For nearly two decades at the end of his eventful life—he died in 1997—Deng was the de facto leader of the PRC. Next to Mao, no one had as big an impact on the country during the second half of the twentieth century.

Deng was the architect of the "Reform and Opening" policies that set the course for China's post-Mao economic surge. He was the man who handled the successful negotiations with Margaret Thatcher that smoothed the way for Hong Kong's July 1, 1997, transition from a British territory to a specially administered part of the PRC. (That date was chosen because it marked the end of Britain's ninety-nine-year lease on the land just across the harbor from Hong Kong Island; the British could have tried to keep the island, which was not leased but had been ceded to them outright, but it would have been isolated and would have had difficulty obtaining basic necessities such as water and electricity.) Deng was also the first Chinese

Communist leader to move away from a personality-cult approach to leadership. Mao had denied that he wanted such a cult, but then did a great deal to help one develop, and Hua Guofeng continued the tradition. Deng cut it off.

Deng's face did not feature prominently on many posters, whereas Mao's had appeared on hundreds (some of which had print runs in the millions); despite Hua Guofeng's relatively short time in power, he too appeared on dozens of propaganda posters.[1] Similarly, while "Long Live Chairman Mao" and "Long Live Chairman Hua" were common slogans at celebratory state rituals before 1979, in Deng's time and since, the term *wansui* ("long live," literally "ten thousand years") has tended to be used only in calls for the continuation of institutions (the CCP), large groups (the people of the PRC), and policies (the "unity of all ethnicities"). In 1984, at the height of Deng's popularity, some students did hold up a banner reading "Hello Xiaoping," an informal form of address, when he reviewed the troops on National Day. There are also some statues honoring him, including a big one in Shenzhen, a city near Hong Kong that he played a key role in transforming from a backwater into a major metropolis when he made it one of the first special economic zones, where elements of capitalism were allowed to take root. But, in general, Deng was seen even at the apex of his authority as the first among equals in an oligarchy rather than as the country's supreme leader.

Throughout the Mao era, Deng was alternately elevated to high posts and demoted in disgrace, sometimes viewed as having a skill at managing the economy that was invaluable but at other times criticized for being too permissive. He was last purged during the Cultural Revolution, when his family also suffered greatly (one of his sons was bullied to the point of falling or jumping off a roof and being crippled for life).

From late 1978 on, Deng was clearly in charge of China, having managed to muscle Hua Guofeng aside after just two years, and a new period, the Reform Era, is said to have begun as soon as his position of supremacy was secure. He remained the most powerful individual in China until his death early in 1997, living long enough to be the most important backer of 1989's June 4th crackdown, which ended weeks of protests in Tiananmen Square and other central plazas across China, but not quite long enough to see Hong Kong become part of the PRC. Officially, however, he was referred to throughout much of his time in power as simply the nation's vice-premier. Additionally, even though during his final years Deng was officially retired, he still exerted great influence from behind the scenes.

Who were Deng's successors?

One thing that Deng had in common with Mao was an inability to fix upon an heir apparent. As with Mao's chosen successors—most notably Lin Biao and Gang of Four member Wang Hongwen—those Deng singled out first rose high in the hierarchy and then fell out of favor. This happened to Hu Yaobang (1915–1989), who was elevated to the lofty post of general secretary of the CCP under Deng but then demoted to the status of a minor official in 1987 for taking too soft a line against student-led protests. This pattern was repeated with Zhao Ziyang (1919–2005), an important ally to Deng in implementing economic reforms before 1987 and Hu's replacement as general secretary. Zhao, however, opposed the hard-line crackdown Deng carried out against the Tiananmen protests and spent the remainder of his life under house arrest. Deng's final heir apparent was Jiang Zemin (1926–), who took over as general secretary in 1989 after Zhao's fall.

However, Jiang was not fully in charge until Deng's death in 1997. Hu Jintao then succeeded Jiang in 2002, in a smooth handover of power. This was supposed to set a precedent for transitions to come, beginning with one that would take place in 2012, after Hu had served two five-year terms. It was not a complete transfer of power, since, like Deng in his final years, Jiang continued to be an influential figure despite having officially retired and relinquished most of his formal posts. Now in his ninth decade, Jiang is still rumored, even after yet another transition, to exert enough influence behind the scenes that current president and general secretary Xi Jinping has targeted many of Jiang's allies within the CCP in an ongoing anti-corruption campaign (about which more below).[2] In contrast to Jiang, Hu has appeared to play a relatively small role in politics, even behind the scenes, since stepping down as general secretary in November 2012.

China's next big transfer of power went far less smoothly than did the one involving Jiang and Hu when, in early 2012, the biggest political scandal in decades hit China. Centering on Bo Xilai and his wife Gu Kailai, it set up conflict and drama ahead of the year's long-anticipated changeover and made Hu's final year as party secretary a rocky one. Bo, party chief of the mega-metropolis of Chongqing and a leading contender for a position on the Politburo Standing Committee, was suddenly purged amid a murder scandal in mid-March (about which more below).

Confusion and chaos appeared to reign at the top of the Chinese political leadership for the next several months. Xi Jinping, the presumptive next party secretary, disappeared from public view for several weeks in late summer, sparking rumors that he had fallen ill or been purged himself. The Eighteenth Party Congress, which most observers had anticipated would be held in September or early October, did not take place until November, allegedly because of backroom squabbles among party elite over which officials would be elevated to the powerful Politburo Standing Committee. Scholars and commentators went into overdrive with their "Pekingology"—the minute analysis of every shift in the winds, however minor, over the leadership compound at Zhongnanhai—anticipating high drama, or even a coup, at the Party congress.

When it did finally take place, though, the meeting went smoothly, with no major last-minute surprises. Xi became the PRC's leader, rising to general secretary in November and becoming president as well in March 2013. The Standing Committee's size was reduced from nine members to seven, but that was expected. Many observers thought Hu, like Jiang, would retain his military posts for a brief period after ceding his civilian ones, but instead these passed immediately to Xi. For all of the Pekingology that went on that fall, the end results were exactly those that had long been predicted.

What defied prediction, though, was how Xi behaved once in power. Knowing little about him before he took control, many observers thought he would either be a colorless figure who would keep from rocking the boat, like his predecessor Hu, or a liberalizer who would follow up Deng's economic reforms (described below) with political ones. The reality would be very different. Xi has moved forcefully against rivals within the elite; developed something closer to a personality cult than has been seen since the time of Mao; and has moved to rein in civil society and activism more forcefully than any leader has since the repressive post-Tiananmen chill that began in June 1989 started to thaw in the early 1990s.

The novelty of certain aspects of Xi's time in power, including the decision at the October 2017 Nineteenth Party Congress to insert Xi's name and references to his ideas into the party constitution, have led some longtime practitioners of Pekingology to argue that it is time to view the PRC as having entered a third major era. There were, according to this line of thinking, the Mao years (1949–1976), followed by the Reform Era that began in the late 1970s, but the latter has now ended. China's current paramount leader and those loyal to him have begun referring to the Nineteenth Party Congress, at which no clear heir apparent to Xi was designated, as inaugurating a glorious "new era" (*xin shidai*) that finds the country surging back to greatness.

Some other China observers, by contrast, feel it is too soon to be sure a new era has started. A third set of people—and we fit into this category—accept the idea that a major shift has occurred, but take a darker view of its implications, emphasizing the moves toward tightening control over society that have been taking place under Xi. We also join with some other analysts in feeling that the endpoint of the Reform Era should be placed earlier than 2017.[3] Xi's moves toward a form of rule that had more trappings of a personality cult than had been common for decades began in 2012. Moreover, the final years of Hu's time in power saw the state more rather than less concerned with issues of control, reversing a trend toward very gradual loosening up that had begun in 1992. It seems clear to us that an important inflection point has been reached, which differentiates today's China sharply from Deng's Reform Era. But it is less easy to pinpoint when exactly this new "Post-Reform Era" (a parallel to the "Post-Mao Era") began.

What exactly did Deng do?

On the international front, in addition to brokering the deal over Hong Kong, Deng Xiaoping's main foreign-policy accomplishment was to normalize relations with Washington, DC. After his 1979 visit to the United States, Deng was viewed by Washington politicians as the only head of a communist party with whom the United States could easily do business. He was responsible as well for the reestablishment of regular relations between Moscow and Beijing in the 1980s. One reason that 1989's Tiananmen protests received such widespread international media coverage, in fact, was that shortly after the protests began Mikhail Gorbachev was in China taking part in a series of high-profile meetings with Deng that were supposed to cement the restoration of close ties between the world's two largest communist states. Deng was not always successful on the international front—a brief but costly war with Vietnam occurred under his watch in 1979—but he brought China back onto the world stage after two decades of Cold War factionalism and isolationism.

Deng's most important legacy is his introduction of a series of bold economic reforms that paved the way for China's three decades of record-breaking growth beginning in the late 1970s. These reforms were intended to temper communist ideology with limited forms of private entrepreneurship, appeals for foreign investment, and a partial reduction of state control over agriculture and industry. The goal was to unleash pent-up entrepreneurial energy, revitalize farming by allowing the most productive farmers to sell some of their yield for profit, and promote "Socialism with Chinese Characteristics," a unique economic system in which the state would still control much of the economy but would allow greater room for free enterprise and decentralization than there had been in the era of Soviet-style five-year plans.

What was the "One-Child" Policy?

While not associated with Deng personally in the way that economic reforms have been, China's so-called One-Child Policy was implemented shortly after he rose to power, in 1979. This birth-control program has lasted long after Deng's death, though it has been modified recently—the policy was tweaked in 2013 and then altered dramatically in 2015.

The name "One-Child Policy," often used in the West, is somewhat misleading, for two reasons. First, the one-child rule was never universally applied. From the start exceptions were made that allowed some couples to have more than a single child, including, for most of the drive's history, non-Han couples. Second, even during the periods of most intense enforcement, it was less a unified national policy than a multifaceted effort to promote a target for population limitation. Local officials had a great deal of discretion over the means by which they reached the birth quotas for their jurisdictions.

The One-Child Policy grew out of fears among the post-Mao 1970s leadership that the country's population was growing at an unsustainable rate and would result in a demographic crisis. Designed to shrink the population and foster economic growth, the basic aim of the policy was to limit the size of Chinese families, by ensuring that most couples had one or at most two children. A mixture of methods was used to achieve this goal, the least coercive of which included persuading people with one or two offspring to have no more. A massive bureaucracy of "population police" was created to monitor and control the fertility of the women under their watch. (For the most part, men sidestepped this oversight, although there were a few locations where vasectomies were the population-control method of choice.)[4]

This policy drew criticism in the West. Some questioned whether, even though China had a baby-boom generation reaching childbearing age in the late 1970s and 1980s (encouraged by Mao, who had pronounced that a great strength of the PRC was its vast number of people), policies this stringent were truly needed to keep the country's population in check. They theorized that rising education levels and national prosperity would have led to a natural reduction in the birthrate.

In addition, opponents of abortion, particularly in the United States (a minority, but a very vocal one), were angered that family-planning workers routinely used the procedure for ending an unwanted pregnancy. The pressure put on local officials to ensure that their communities met strict birth quotas meant that some women were coerced into having abortions.

Many Americans condemned the Chinese government for interfering in matters they thought of as private, as occurred when "period police" monitored whether women were menstruating and when bureaucrats dictated when exactly couples could start a family and how many children they should have.[5] There were also disturbing echoes of eugenic ideas in some of the propaganda that accompanied the policy initially, which referred to the need for fewer but "better" children—though this was partly offset when exemptions to have additional offspring were granted to China's fifty-five officially recognized *shaoshu minzu* (literally, minority nationalities; i.e., everyone who is not ethnically Han Chinese).

Over the span of thirty-five years, a combination of factors—the One-Child Policy, increased educational opportunities for women, and the rising cost of rearing children—succeeded in lowering China's birthrate. In fact, the birthrate fell *too* much, and a different set of demographic concerns face today's Chinese leadership. The country's population is aging and its labor force shrinking, a trend expected to accelerate in decades to come. In a belated attempt to mitigate these future problems, the government first loosened the One-Child Policy in 2013, then revised it altogether in late 2015.

Couples are now permitted—even encouraged—to have two children, although it is not yet clear how many will take advantage of this new opportunity. For many urbanites, the high costs of caring for and educating children makes stopping at one a pragmatic decision. And many couples in their mid-thirties, who were born at the beginning of the policy, face the prospect of caring for four elderly parents with no siblings to assist them and a weak elder-care infrastructure (nursing homes, although becoming more numerous in China, are still rare, as traditional Confucian ideals call for children to care for their parents in old age). Given other demands on their time, money, and energy, it is uncertain if young couples will produce the baby boom that China's leaders hope to see.[6]

Was female infanticide encouraged to help limit population size?

No—though sometimes foreign observers, Americans particularly, have thought this was the case.

That said, the early 1980s did see a resurgence of female infanticide (a practice that was known in pre-revolutionary China but diminished rapidly after 1949), and there were also sex-selective abortions by couples determined to have at least one son. The combination of these two things led to skewed sex ratios in some rural locales, where many more boys than girls survive the first years of childhood—a phenomenon that could have profound social consequences.[7]

Misunderstanding arises when Chinese female infanticide and sex-selective abortions have been presented as *part* of the One-Child Policy, which they were not. These actions, and husbands' (or in-laws') abuse of women who bear daughters instead of sons, are better understood as acts of *resistance* to the One-Child Policy. After all, one of its key tenets, as evidenced by the constant use of happy-looking lone infant daughters on posters extolling the virtues of small families, was that couples should be just as delighted to have a female child as a male.[8]

When family members showed displeasure with female children or, in the most extreme cases, ended their lives, they were going against—not conforming to—dictates from on high. The Chinese government can be taken to task for failing to fight hard enough to counter the preference for sons, and some policies have inadvertently worked to reinforce the bias toward male children. Most notably, in a time of increasing privatization of agriculture, in a country where it has never stopped being the norm for rural brides to move to their husbands' households, there is a strong economic incentive to have a child who is likely to bring labor power into the family via marriage. A woman, on the other hand, takes her labor with her when she marries, so that her labor power benefits her in-laws more than it does her own parents. There is a difference, however, between saying that the Chinese authorities *could have done much more* to minimize female infanticide, or that their policies inadvertently contributed to its rise, and saying that it *was an element of* government policy.

How is Deng viewed now?

Had he died before 1989, Deng would have gone down in history in both the West and in China as a celebrated figure. He was admired for his pragmatism (in contrast to Mao, who emphasized ideological purity, Deng claimed he didn't care if a cat was a "black cat or a white cat" because if it caught mice, it was a "good cat") and for slogans that moved away from a focus on class struggle ("to get rich is glorious" was another of his best-known slogans). *Time* magazine selected Deng as its "Man of the Year" not once but twice, in 1978 and 1985. Only one previous Chinese leader, Chiang Kai-shek, who had been a personal favorite of Time-Life's chief, Henry Luce, had been given that honor even once—and Chiang had to share it with his spouse, Song Meiling, the only time that a "Man and Wife of the Year" were recognized by *Time*. Though there were many parts of Deng's policies that stopped short of representing a full embrace of capitalism, he was often described as creating a China that was more capitalist than communist.

Currently, although Deng is officially regarded in China as a man who did great things for the nation, his international reputation is mixed. On the positive side, Deng instituted economic reforms that paved the way for China's transformation from a Third World economy to the world's second-biggest economy by GDP. Foreign observers, however, disapproved of Deng's go-slow approach to political reforms, which did little to expand freedom of expression or other civil rights. Additionally, while Deng elevated both China's GDP and international reputation, he violently crushed dissident movements, including the Democracy Wall protests of the late 1970s and, even more importantly, the Tiananmen protests of 1989. Deng, like Mao, remains a complicated figure whose legacy is impossible to summarize in a single soundbite.[9]

What was the Democracy Wall movement?

The Democracy Wall movement was named for the place in Beijing where protesters began to put up manifestos, poems, and other documents of dissent in the fall of 1978. The aims and rhetoric of the activists varied widely, as many were inspired by Marxist ideas or at least by critical strains within the communist world (e.g., reformist calls from other communist nations for a check on the tendency for cadres to become an elitist "new class" within state socialist settings), while others were influenced by liberal concepts. The *minzhu* in the 1970s' *minzhuqiang* (meaning "democracy wall," a term first used for a protest space in the late 1940s and then again during the Hundred Flowers period of the late 1950s) could, in other words, stand for many things, but primarily it expressed a desire for rulers to listen to the people.

At first, Deng seemed to think that it was a good thing that citizens were venting their hopes and frustrations. By the end of 1979, however, in a sort of replay of the Hundred Flowers campaign's conclusion, the government labeled the protests dangerous and imprisoned some of the boldest authors of posters.

The best-known Democracy Wall participant is Wei Jingsheng (1950–), who was imprisoned for many years for his activism and now lives in the United States as a political exile. His famous poster played upon Deng's policy of Four Modernizations, which emphasized the need for China to modernize agriculture, industry, technology, and defense. China also needed, Wei insisted, a Fifth Modernization (the name of his manifesto): democratic reform.

What happened at Tiananmen Square in 1989?

Although the crushing of the Democracy Wall movement signaled that Deng would not tolerate excessive criticism of the CCP and its government, more and more Chinese felt the freedom to express their grievances and hopes during the decade that followed. Students held protests in several Chinese cities in December 1986 (the biggest demonstrations occurred in Shanghai), a wave of campus activism that ended with Beijing students making a New Year's Day 1987 march to Tiananmen Square. These demonstrations were rooted in a complex mix of goals. The youths involved wanted more personal freedom and were frustrated with various aspects of university life, from compulsory calisthenics to the low quality of cafeteria food, and they wanted campus leaders to be chosen via open elections rather than being handpicked by the CCP.

There were some scattered protests in 1988, but a true resurgence of activism did not come until April 1989. Beijing students planned to commemorate the eightieth anniversary of China's greatest student movement on May 4, but that might have amounted to no more than an isolated symbolic action, if an event with profound implications for the political scene had not taken place. This was the mid-April death of Hu Yaobang, who had become a hero to the students when Deng Xiaoping criticized and demoted him for taking a soft line on the 1986–1987 protests.

Hu's death opened a window of opportunity for Beijing's university students: when Hu died he was still an official, albeit not a high-ranking one, so the state could hardly prevent people from gathering to mourn his passing. By April 22, the day of Hu's memorial service, tens of thousands of students had assembled in Tiananmen Square. They attempted to present a petition outlining their grievances to Premier Li Peng, who refused to accept it. The students began remarking what a shame it was when good men died, while bad ones lived on and stayed in control. Over the following days, the crowds at Tiananmen and elsewhere swelled. Although the 1989 protests are chiefly associated with Beijing, where a million people rallied at the movement's peak, large crowds, in some cases hundreds of thousands strong, took to the streets and central squares of other cities such as Shanghai, Xi'an, and Guangzhou.[10]

One key difference from the 1986–1987 demonstrations was that, by the time the Tiananmen movement reached its apex in mid-May, it was much more than just a student upsurge. By then, the most important demonstrations involved members of many social groups. Workers were particularly numerous in marches, drawn to the cause partly by the fact that though students made democracy one of their watchwords they spent as much energy attacking the leadership for growing corrupt and failing to spread the fruits of economic development. This criticism echoed powerfully throughout Chinese society at a time when inflation was rampant and, while there were some cases of entrepreneurs without official ties striking it rich, many of the people getting wealthy were the children of top leaders and those with high-level official connections.

Support peaked after students staged a hunger strike, an act that had special potency since lavish banquets had become a symbol of officials' selfish behavior. Tapping into a longstanding Chinese tradition of educated youths laying their bodies on the line to protect the nation, the hunger strikers sought to show that they were more committed to the good of the country than were Deng and other party oligarchs.

By early June, the movement had lost most of its momentum, and it is possible that the protesters would have left Tiananmen Square on their own in time. Li Peng and other hard-liners in the leadership, however, were not interested in waiting for the protests to fizzle out, and they persuaded Deng to turn away from the moderates in the government, who were championed by General Secretary Zhao Ziyang. Almost thirty years after the events of 1989, we still only have a partial understanding of how Deng came to share Li's point of view and send troops to clear Tiananmen Square on the night of June 3, in a military action that lasted into the early hours of June 4—the date that is now most closely associated with the year's bloody crackdown on dissent.

After darkness fell on June 3, PLA units moved through the streets of Beijing, converging on the square from multiple directions. Along the way, soldiers fired on Beijing residents who attempted to halt their advance. Reaching Tiananmen Square, the PLA units surrounded the remaining protesters; leaders of the demonstrations negotiated with the soldiers, and students began to leave the square at gunpoint but not under gunfire. By dawn on June 4, Tiananmen Square was empty of protesters for the first time in more than six weeks.

Although it's common for Westerners to call the violence of June 3–4 the "Tiananmen Square Massacre," very few people died in the square itself (some eyewitnesses sympathetic to the protests even claim that none were killed in that precise locale). There is incontrovertible proof, however, that many people were killed on the streets surrounding the giant plaza. This geographical detail means that Tiananmen Square Massacre is an inaccurate term, which is open to criticism by the CCP, so we find it more fitting to call it by other names, though not "Tiananmen Incident," which glosses over the fact that there was a large death toll. In Chinese, it is simply referred to by a pair of numbers, six (*liu*) and four (*si*), so reference to the killings of June 4th will do.

It is also worth noting the confusion surrounding the most enduring image of June 1989: the photo of a solitary man (most likely a worker, not a student) standing off against a line of tanks on June 5. Its fame has led many foreigners to believe that most of those who died in early June were crushed by tanks, when the main cause of death was injuries from automatic gunfire. There is no official death toll, and estimates differ wildly; there is clear evidence, though, that hundreds of people were killed. Some students died, but the majority of those slain, both in Beijing and in the western city of Chengdu, where a massacre also occurred in early June, were workers and other ordinary inhabitants. A very small number of soldiers, who became the only martyrs recognized in official Chinese government accounts of events, were killed by crowds as well.[11]

Although mentions of 1989 are extraordinarily rare in the Chinese press or government publications today, when it has spoken of the events of June 4th the government has insisted that there was no "massacre" at all. It has declared instead that the event was simply an effort by soldiers—who showed great restraint when dealing with crowds, and in some cases paid for this by being burned alive in their vehicles—to put an end to a counter-revolutionary riot. This so-called riot, the government claimed, disrupted life in China's capital, threatened the stability of the nation, and, if left unchecked, could have sent the country spiraling into the kind of disorder that had characterized the Cultural Revolution era. That view of events has been labeled in the West, quite appropriately, the "Big Lie" about 1989. Only a few soldiers were killed and the government exaggerated greatly when raising the bogeyman of the Cultural Revolution, given that the protests of 1989 were largely nonviolent.

The PRC government has implemented a kind of enforced national amnesia concerning the early June massacres, and those who seek to talk about it—the "Tiananmen Mothers," for example, a group of now-elderly women whose children died in the crackdown—are surveilled and silenced.[12] Search terms related to the protests and crackdown—even, at times, the numerical combination of six and four—are blocked on the Chinese Internet. As the June 4th anniversary comes around every spring, government scrutiny of activists increases and foreign journalists are harassed as they head to Tiananmen Square to report on security measures in place. A massive candlelight vigil does take place in Hong Kong on June 4th each year, but its meaning has shifted: now it has less to do with commemorating the victims of 1989 and is more about expressing discontent with Beijing's rule over the territory (about which more below). The CCP has proven itself determined to prevent any sort of open discussion about the events of 1989, and while the topic continues to be discussed in Hong Kong publications, in November 2017 a pro-Beijing education official announced plans to excise comments on the protests and June 4th massacre from local textbooks.

Why hasn't the Chinese government changed its line on Tiananmen?

Many supporters of the Tiananmen movement hoped that within a few years the Chinese government would reassess the protests of 1989. In 1976, a similar set of demonstrations, which also centered on Tiananmen Square and which were also triggered in part by the death of an admired official—in that case, Zhou Enlai—were initially dubbed counter-revolutionary riots but then, after Deng's rise, reassessed as a patriotic struggle. Relatives of slain students and workers, and human rights activists around the world, have pushed for a similar reassessment of the protests of 1989, but this has not come to pass. In the absence of such a reversal, those who attempt to call attention to the events and victims of June 4th find themselves harassed and sometimes detained by the Public Security Bureau. School textbooks, newspapers, and scholarly works cannot pass the scrutiny of censors and get approved for publication if they discuss the Tiananmen protests and subsequent state violence.

One reason for the lack of a reassessment is that there has not been the same kind of shift within the CCP leadership as that which occurred in the aftermath of the 1976 protests. Deng's 1978 rise signaled a dramatic turnaround, and he could logically interpret the 1976 protests as a precocious signal of support for his eventual assumption of power.

The situation relating to June 4th is very different. Indeed, while there are various tensions within the current leadership, all high-ranking individuals in power today consider themselves to be closely associated with Deng and his policies. As a result, they resist reappraising the massacre for fear that doing so may seem a repudiation of Deng's vision, and by extension undermine their own political legitimacy.

Another reason may be that images of tanks rolling through Beijing's central districts are simply too potentially delegitimizing to allow, even at a time when many Chinese might be willing to accept the notion that maintaining social order then had provided the framework for the economic boom to come. One of the central stories that the CCP tells about itself is that its armed forces played a crucial role in fighting invading armies. This part of its narrative has become more important than ever in the present nationalistic period, when some of the once-favored legitimation stories, such as how post-1949 China reduced the gap between rich and poor, have lost their valence. Footage of the people of Beijing being subdued by PLA armored vehicles and soldiers firing automatic weapons, by contrast, makes the forces of the CCP look a great deal like an army intent on occupying, not liberating, the Chinese capital.

What effect did the fall of other communist governments have on China?

It would be easy to assume that the international climate during the last years of the previous century and the first years of this one was not conducive to regimes founded upon the ideas of Karl Marx. Some have claimed that the events of 1989 proved Marx wrong, once and for all. Others suggest that Marx's ideas with regard to what we today refer to as globalization were incredibly prescient.[13] Whatever the case may be, recent trends in world affairs, even if bad for Marxism per se, have made it easier for the CCP to defend its distinctive version of this creed.

Consider, for example, how well events of the 1990s fit in with the regime's assertion that a strong state and emphasis on stability best serves China's national interests. For Beijing propagandists trying to argue this point of view, the Yugoslavian descent into chaos was a godsend. The collapse of order in that part of southeastern Europe allowed the CCP to point out, if not in these precise terms, that no matter how dissatisfied someone might be to live in a *communist* state, there was a less appealing alternative out there: living in a *post-communist* country such as those in the war-torn region that Tito had once governed. Furthermore, after NATO forces intervened to protect Kosovo, the CCP was able to claim that a post-communist era involved not just economic collapse and widespread violence, but a loss of independence—an especially sore point in a nation that long suffered from imperialist encroachments.

The year 1989 presented a major challenge to the CCP, one that many thought at the time it would not be able to withstand: the protest wave that brought a million people into the streets of Beijing and onto the capital's biggest plaza and drew tens or hundreds of thousands into the central districts of scores of other cities. The party survived, but only after Deng and the other oligarchs of his generation took a series of drastic steps. Specifically, they ordered the June 4th crackdown; they carried out a campaign of mass arrests; and they demoted Zhao Ziyang and placed him under house arrest. The other key event of 1989 was the rise to power of Jiang Zemin, the Shanghai leader who proved his skills to the oligarchs by taking a firm stand against the protests and restoring order in his city using only limited force.

The year was also a challenging one for Deng and his allies because communist regimes fell in Budapest, Bucharest, and other European capitals. In 1989, the Solidarity party rose to power in Poland (winning its first election on the very day that PLA soldiers were firing on civilians in Beijing), the Velvet Revolution occurred in Prague, and the Berlin Wall crumbled. And though the Soviet Union remained intact and under communist rule, its days seemed numbered.

In the wake of these developments, it became the conventional wisdom outside of China that the group responsible for the June 4th violence could not possibly hold onto power for long. The catchphrase was that the "End of History" had arrived and soon there would be no communist states left. Throughout the 1990s, the notion that the CCP was unlikely to survive remained an article of faith for many Western journalists, academics, and policymakers. As the CCP endured into the twenty-first century, though, more and more foreign observers acknowledged it was doubtful that the "Leninist extinction" (another phrase from the Western literature of the time) would affect Beijing.[14]

The tide has shifted even more recently. Many now agree that, barring unexpected events, the CCP is likely to survive for some time to come. In fact, it can now claim, playing on a phrase attributed to Mark Twain, that reports of its death have been greatly exaggerated. Indeed, CCP leaders might not mind being linked to a line associated with that particular US author, given that he was a sharp critic of US imperialism and even wrote an editorial early in his career calling attention to the unfairness of the treaty-port system in China.

How did China's rulers avoid falling prey to the Leninist extinction?

One reason that Deng and Jiang were able to prove the skeptics wrong in the 1990s has already been noted: they could point to the traumas experienced by some formerly communist countries. Their twenty-first-century successors have continued to do this, while also making corollary efforts to highlight and amplify any bad news relating to non-communist countries where dictators or authoritarian groups have been overthrown. The Chinese state media made a great deal, for example, of how chaotic, dangerous, and strife-ridden Iraq became after the United States toppled Saddam Hussein, as well as the instability experienced by several countries in Africa and the Middle East (e.g., Libya and Egypt) after the 2011 Arab Spring wave of protests and revolutions there. Here are four other factors worth stressing when seeking to understand the surprising longevity of the CCP.

First, the regime has made great and largely successful efforts to co-opt traditionally restive or particularly troublesome groups. Entrepreneurs who were frustrated by getting too little respect from the authorities and having too little influence in how China was run were among those who supported the 1989 protests; they are now welcomed into the CCP. Although intellectuals go through periods (including the current moment) of feeling more constraints from above, in recent decades they have regularly enjoyed access to a much wider array of books and journal articles and been able to travel abroad more easily than their Soviet bloc counterparts of old. This has helped minimize, though not completely eradicate, their disaffection with the CCP, which led so many of them to support the Tiananmen protests. Additionally, the government has stopped micromanaging daily life on university campuses, which has similarly lessened the discontent of students, a group that played a crucial role in the 1989 protests.

Second, the government has followed a post-1989 strategy of patriotic education, emphasizing the CCP's historical ties to anti-imperialist movements. Like all of the other main enduring communist party regimes (including those of North Korea, Vietnam, and Cuba) and unlike many of those that fell in 1989 (including those in Poland and Hungary), China's came to power via a struggle for independence. Also like the heads of those other regimes, China's leaders make overstated claims about the role their organization played in saving their country from imperialists and underplay the contributions of other groups. Yet all the communist organizations still in power are justified in asserting ties to nationalist risings. In the Chinese case, the CCP's role in fighting the Japanese in World War II is celebrated whenever the regime's legitimacy needs burnishing, and China's role in the Korean War (presented as an effort to free a neighboring government from foreign domination) is also commemorated.[15]

Third, the government has worked hard to raise the standard of living and availability of consumer goods within its leading cities. This is something that none of the communist regimes that fell late in the last century managed to do, and such failure helped bring about their collapse. Frustration relating to abstract issues such as freedom of speech contributed to dissatisfaction with the communist regimes that fell in 1989, but material issues contributed, too. People living in East Berlin, for example, knew that on the other side of the Berlin Wall, in what had formerly been part of the same city, one could shop at much more attractive department stores and supermarkets. Comparable things could have been said in 1989 about the contrast between Shanghai and capitalist Taipei in Taiwan (today that difference is gone, if not reversed). Europe's state socialist regimes claimed that they were not only morally superior to their capitalist rivals but could also compete with them materially. They could not, and it cost them. China's leadership has done a better job at—quite literally—delivering the goods.

Fourth, the CCP leadership has adopted a flexible strategy toward protests that has prevented new broad-based movements from taking shape on the mainland. Conflagrations are common, as evident from official reports that that there are tens of thousands of protests every year in China. Through various means, however, the government has managed to temper the unrest and prevent another crisis. Whereas Mao warned that a "single spark" could start a "prairie fire,"[16] his successors have developed sophisticated strategies of allowing some localized eruptions of discontent but preventing these from triggering large conflagrations, which one scholar has likened to the "controlled burn" methods of foresters.[17]

How has the government responded to protests since 1989?

The Chinese authorities have used harsh measures to suppress some kinds of unrest and gone to extraordinary lengths to limit awareness of these actions. But the government has generally taken a less draconian stance toward other sorts of resistance, at times even punishing local officials who have been criticized by protesters.[18] This point deserves close scrutiny, since the Western press gives so much attention to patterns of dissent and moments of upheaval in the PRC, and because government response to a particular protest is far from straightforward.

The calculus that tips the official response toward or away from outright repression involves a number of factors. Equally complicated is the decision about whether there will be a complete, or merely partial, effort to block information about what has occurred. Because of what happened during the Tiananmen Square protests and an awareness of the importance of cross-class protests in places such as Poland in the 1980s, the CCP views movements involving members of more than one occupational or economic group as particularly dangerous. Also key is how geographically dispersed dissenters are: purely local events—ranging from small-scale tax strikes to neighborhood discussions of new chemical plants—tend to be treated more leniently. A third factor that influences the severity of the regime's response, both toward protesters and toward domestic and foreign journalists seeking to cover events, is how well organized dissenters seem to be. The less evidence of careful coordination, the more likely the response will be to mollify crowds rather than strike terror into them—and the more likely reporters will be allowed to cover the event.

For example, when the Arab Spring protest movement broke out in early 2011, the PRC government moved swiftly to ensure that nothing similar would take place in China. Aside from some anonymous postings online that called for "Jasmine" protests (a name borrowed from that year's revolution in Tunisia), there was little sign that any demonstrations were even planned. Still, Chinese authorities initiated a widespread Internet crackdown and arrested a number of humanrights lawyers and activists, including the prominent artist Ai Weiwei (about whom more below). Chinese leaders apparently feared the threat of a wide-ranging protest movement that could appeal to many different social groups and spark a repeat of the 1989 protests.[19]

For a time, it seemed that the village of Wukan in Guangdong Province would provide an example of how local protests can sometimes garner government approval rather than censure. In 2011, Wukan residents complained that their local CCP representatives were illegally seizing and selling villagers' land without providing fair compensation. One of the leading protesters then died under mysterious circumstances while in police custody, further escalating tensions, and villagers soon

drove the CCP cadres out of town. Guangdong authorities initially blockaded Wukan, surrounding the village with security forces. Soon after, however, they began negotiating with
the villagers and eventually reached a settlement: Wukan
residents would be allowed to elect a new village party chief
and the standoff between the province and protesters would
end. For the next several years, the "Wukan Experiment"
served as the primary example of a Chinese protest with a
positive outcome.

In mid-2016, however, Wukan villagers once again rose
up, renewing their claims of stolen land, and Lin Zuluan, the
elected party chief, declared that he would lead the fight for
justice. No longer willing to tolerate expressions of discontent
from Lin and his troublemaking village, higher-level officials
arrested him on charges of corruption and bribery. This move
triggered months of pro-Lin demonstrations in Wukan. In
September, the regional government decided to put an end
to the rebellion and sent in riot police to secure order in the
village. Wukan, once a symbol of the remaining space for
people power in China, instead became one more example of
the Chinese government's intolerance toward protest when it
aims too high or garners too much attention.[20]

Three additional elements in government responses to
protest are worth noting. First, geography helps determine
whether it will take a hard or soft line. The government will
use force much more swiftly when unrest occurs in frontier
zones, such as Tibet and Xinjiang, where large percentages of
the population do not belong to the majority Han group. It is
also in these areas that economic grievances and anger associated with ethnic and religious divides make for a particularly
volatile combination.

Second, the regime's relatively lenient treatment of some
protests can be interpreted as a sign of self-confidence. One
political scientist argues that it is a mistake to treat reports that
many protests occur as an indicator of weakness. It may be
a sign of regime *strength* when the government admits that

protests are occurring and sometimes even allows people to let off steam without responding harshly.[21]

Finally, it seems that protesters in China have the greatest chance of achieving their objectives when they strive to achieve very specific and narrow goals, point out that what they seek is simply for the CCP to fulfill the concrete promises it has made to its citizens, or do both of these things. Disputes over fair compensation for land taken by the government, for example, are likely to be resolved relatively smoothly, as was initially the case in Wukan, and the same is true of Not in My Backyard (NIMBY) environmental protests that aim simply to have a noxious factory closed or built somewhere other than a specific place. On the other hand, protesters who pursue bigger, more abstract goals—such as democracy or religious freedom—more frequently find themselves arrested and tried on charges of "inciting subversion of state power," a vague accusation that the government can use however it wishes.

What is the CCP's stance toward religion in China?

The CCP established the PRC as an atheist state, but this does not mean that religion has been banned in China since 1949. There have been periods of extreme repression (such as the Cultural Revolution decade), while at other times more space is allowed for expressions of belief. Officially, the PRC recognizes five faiths: Buddhism, Daoism, Islam, Protestant Christianity, and Catholicism. The fact that a religion is on this list, however, does not mean its adherents are free to practice as they wish. Nor are all treated equally.

When religion and ethnic identity overlap, as in Buddhist Tibet and Muslim Xinjiang, the Chinese government is especially insistent that it dictate the terms of religious practice. The government fears "splittist" (*fenliezhuyi*, a Chinese term referring to groups seeking independence) movements in these two regions and hopes that keeping a tight grip on religious expression will prevent such fragmentation. Tibetan

Buddhists are not permitted to demonstrate allegiance to the exiled Dalai Lama, for example, and government-run monasteries display portraits of Chinese leaders instead. In recent years, Muslim residents in Xinjiang have seen their observation of the Ramadan fast impeded, and the government has discouraged men from growing beards and women from wearing headscarves.

In other cases, however, the government's wariness of religion does not extend to such extreme practices. "House churches," small Protestant or Catholic congregations that gather for worship in private homes, sometimes find themselves the targets of crackdowns but at other times are permitted to continue without incident.[22] Protestant Christianity has seen tremendous growth in the past several decades, especially in the countryside, and now claims about 60 million followers in China—a small percentage in a country with a population of 1.6 billion, to be sure, but not an insignificant number of believers in an officially atheist state.

Roman Catholicism has traveled a rockier road. Catholics look to the Vatican-based pope as the head of their church, but the early PRC government was unwilling to allow foreign control of a religion within its borders. In 1951, the PRC severed ties to the Vatican and established the Chinese Catholic Patriotic Association (CCPA) to oversee the practice of the faith. The Vatican does not recognize government-run congregations, or bishops appointed by the CCPA, and has maintained diplomatic relations with Taiwan rather than Beijing. There are, however, about six million "underground" Catholics who deny the CCPA's authority and express loyalty to the Vatican and the pope. In recent years, the Vatican and Beijing have attempted to mend this rift, and there are frequent reports that the two sides are close to a rapprochement.[23]

In addition, many Chinese are adherents of still other religions, some old (Daoism) and others new (*qigong* sects, whose followers engage in gentle exercise, breathing practices, and meditation to cultivate the self). But if people begin practicing religions that do not fall into one of the five officially recognized faiths, they risk being accused of being members of an "evil cult" (*xiejiao*). The most notorious example of this happened with practitioners of a movement known as Falun Gong.

Why and how has the CCP suppressed the Falun Gong movement?

A campaign of repression that has particularly baffled foreign observers is that which the regime undertook to crush the Falun Gong sect beginning in 1999. Likewise, the resoluteness of China's policy toward the group since the suppression perplexes foreigners. When the crackdown began, Falun Gong adherents had never engaged in violent protest. Indeed, to many outsiders, the group appeared to be nothing more than part of a spiritual movement that involved the practice of meditation and *qigong* exercises. While Falun Gong's leader, Li Hongzhi, professed some particularly unusual ideas, such as claims to powers that many Westerners would consider akin to magical, and a version of scientific facts many would dub superstitions, the Falun Gong did not have a political agenda. It was seen as a threat because its adherents came from all walks of life (even some CCP officials joined it); it was popular throughout the country (cells formed in many cities); and it showed a capability for coordinated action. This capability became manifest in April 1999, when ten thousand protesters assembled outside Zhongnanhai and staged a sit-in, demanding an end to official criticism of the group. This demonstration of people power frightened top government officials; Falun Gong was quickly declared an evil cult and hundreds of its practitioners arrested and allegedly subject to vicious treatment.[24] In the nearly two decades since the crackdown began, the PRC government has kept up its campaign against the practice of Falun Gong. The religion's supporters outside the country (including a large number in the United

States) have proven skilled counter-propagandists, arguing their cause through demonstrations, publications, and cultural performances.[25]

The group's size and reach are not the only reasons for the campaign against Falun Gong. A leading scholar of the subject stresses the ideological challenge that Falun Gong posed to the CCP even before it began to present the party as an evil organization (which only occurred after the crackdown against its members began). He argues that the CCP was threatened by Li's novel fusion of Chinese traditions and modern "science," for the party claims a monopoly on defining what it means to be both Chinese and modern via the "scientific" socialism of Marx.[26]

There are other reasons why the CCP response to Falun Gong represents a special case. For example, during imperial times, Chinese regimes were sometimes weakened or overthrown by millenarian religious movements, including some that began as quiescent self-help sects. Additionally, the party is especially concerned about protests that have ties with charismatic figures, and Li would surely be one. That said, the CCP response still illustrates the general pattern described above of struggles being treated as most serious when they are multi-class, geographically widespread, and well organized.

Which Chinese artists and writers are deemed "dissidents"?

One common mistake that many non-Chinese make is to assume that those engaged in creative activities are either dissidents (who challenge the government and end up in prison or in exile) or loyalists (who follow the regime's line, whether out of belief or fear). In fact, there have always been and still are people in the middle. Since Xi Jinping's ascension to power, however, even they have found themselves targets of the government's crackdown on dissent.

There are those who make their careers doing work designed to shore up and promote the policies of China's current leaders. And on the opposite end of the spectrum are those who openly confront the authorities and at times seem to be daring the state to silence them. But most Chinese fall somewhere between these extremes.

Lingering Cold War assumptions tempt Westerners to assume that there are no critical intellectuals in state socialist countries, but in China they certainly exist. They may not directly challenge the authority of the CCP yet they do criticize aspects of the established order. Many artists and writers operate in a gray zone, where they bend or even flout the rules to avoid harsh government condemnation, but do not confront the government directly. Instead, they make judgment calls about how far they can push before the authorities push back. In particular, some writers evade the censorship associated with official publishing channels by publishing their work on the Internet. Others, such as novelist and essayist Yu Hua (1960–), either publish their more controversial works in Hong Kong and Taiwan, or arrange for English-language versions to appear in foreign publications. Such avenues allow these writers to remain relatively unscathed while living on the mainland.[27]

Someone who might fit into the more conventional Western image of a dissident is avant-garde artist Ai Weiwei (1957–), who lived in New York for over a decade before returning to China in 1993 and who seems to delight in provoking the Chinese government. At one point, he was an artistic consultant on the Bird's Nest Stadium constructed for the Beijing Olympics, but he then denounced the games as propaganda for the CCP. Ai attracted the most government displeasure, though, when he began investigating the deaths of over five thousand schoolchildren who perished as a result of poorly constructed schools that collapsed in a devastating earthquake that hit Sichuan Province in 2008. Ai listed the children's names on his blog, which was then shut down by the authorities. Taking to Twitter, Ai continued speaking out against the government. In the spring of 2011, amid a broader move against lawyers, activists, and outspoken intellectuals in the wake of the Arab Spring, security forces arrested Ai and held him for alleged "economic crimes." (He was later charged with income tax evasion.) Detained for over two months, Ai was then permitted to return to his Beijing home. Although he is no longer under house arrest and is now allowed to travel outside the country, and indeed spends much of his time abroad, the unpredictable Ai remains closely watched by the Chinese government.

When Mo Yan (1955–) won the Nobel Prize in Literature in 2012, some commentators used the contrast between his career and Ai's to chide the Swedish judges for making a foolish choice. Whereas Ai's art challenged the state, they claimed, Mo's abetted it. Whereas Ai was censored and bullied, Mo was lauded and served as a vice chairman of the official Writer's Association. There are crucial differences between the two, which Mo himself underscored in some of the statements he made after winning the prize. He claimed in one, for example, that censorship could benefit rather than harm artists. It is also worth noting, though, that some of Mo's writings have veered at least tentatively into the gray zone, if not as daringly as those of Yu Hua (also a member, though not a vice chairman, of the Writer's Association). While Mo is no dissident, his writings are not devoid of social critique. He can be caustic about the corrosive effects of government corruption on communities, albeit taking aim at local officials only—a far safer target than national ones.[28] Mo has stayed far enough inside the confines of the safe zone to be celebrated by the Chinese leadership for his Nobel Prize, a story very different from that of the PRC's previous Nobel winner, Liu Xiaobo.

Who was Liu Xiaobo?

Liu Xiaobo (1955–2017) had been an activist in China for two decades before many in the West ever heard his name when he was awarded the Nobel Peace Prize in 2010. In the 1980s, Liu was a rising star in academia, renowned for his pathbreaking literary criticism. His academic career came to an end, though, when he joined the Tiananmen protests and emerged as one of the leaders of the moderate faction that wanted to leave the square peacefully. Liu was arrested soon after June 4th and imprisoned for almost two years. Resuming his work as an outspoken political activist and writer upon his release, Liu was repeatedly detained and placed under house arrest. On December 25, 2009, he was sentenced to an eleven-year term for "inciting subversion of state power," a charge brought about by his role in composing *Charter 08* the year before. Liu and other dissidents took the inspiration for this document from Václav Havel's *Charter 77*. In their charter, Liu and others asked the government for democratic reforms, an independent judiciary, and freedom of expression. Circulated online, the petition received thousands of signatures.

Liu was the first PRC citizen to win a Nobel Prize, but the Chinese government expressed no joy at the news. Authorities denounced the award and relations between China and Norway grew chilly (though the Nobel committee is an independent organization not under the control of the Norwegian government). Nineteen countries with ties to China—including Russia, Cuba, Iraq, and Venezuela—boycotted the award ceremony in Oslo. The PRC also prevented the participation of Liu's wife and friends in the ceremony by refusing to let them exit the country. After the chairman of the prize committee read the citation honoring Liu, the audience gave an extended standing ovation to the empty chair where Liu was meant to have sat.[29]

With his eleven-year sentence beginning in 2009, Liu Xiaobo was expected to remain in prison until 2020. In late June 2017, however, prison officials announced that Liu had been diagnosed with advanced liver cancer. Although Liu was transferred to a hospital, he remained under detention and was permitted only a limited number of visitors—including his wife, Liu Xia, who had been held under house arrest in Beijing since Liu received the Nobel Prize.

Liu Xiaobo told visiting family members that he wished to be taken abroad to receive medical treatment, and for several weeks human rights organizations and world leaders called on the Chinese government to honor his request. Their pleas received no response. On July 13, 2017, Liu passed away, the first Nobel Peace Prize winner to die in state custody since Carl von Ossietzky perished under the Nazi regime in 1938.[30]

Who is Chen Guangcheng?

Since the 1990s, there have been in China activist lawyers who generally work within the system, yet take up cases for people struggling to call attention to specific abuses by local officials. (Likewise, members of various single-issue NGOs publicize what they see as flawed government policies relating to topics such as AIDS or the environment, yet do not advocate any radical change in government.) Those activists have always walked a fine line, but until the most recent crackdown on civil society under Xi Jinping, the authorities often permitted them to continue their work, albeit under the watchful gaze of Public Security Bureau officials.

Perhaps the activist lawyer whose name will be most familiar to American readers is the self-taught, blind lawyer Chen Guangcheng (1971–). Working as a "barefoot lawyer" on behalf of others in his small Shandong Province village, Chen filed lawsuits and organized opposition to forced abortions and other extreme methods of enforcing the One-Child Policy. He was jailed from 2006 to 2010, then placed under house arrest until April 2012, when he escaped and fled to the US embassy in Beijing. After several weeks of negotiations, the Chinese government allowed him to leave the country and enroll as a special student at the law school of New York University (NYU). The following year, however, Chen accused the university of bowing to Chinese government pressure in forcing him to leave the school and the housing his family had been provided; NYU countered that it had only ever offered Chen a one-year fellowship. After this bitter and public breakup, Chen largely faded from view, aside from a brief emergence in 2015 to publicize his memoir; he now has fellowships and advisory positions at a conservative think tank and Catholic University.[31] Although Chen has spoken in the past of his hopes to return to China and continue his work there, government repression of civil society activism has increased in recent years, making this highly unlikely.

Who are the Feminist Five?

The case that has come to serve as shorthand for the PRC government's increased repression of civil society under Xi Jinping is that of the Feminist Five, arrested in 2015. That year, activists based in several different Chinese cities planned to hold a protest on March 8 (International Women's Day) that involved handing out stickers and leaflets decrying the prevalence of sexual harassment on public transit. Before the protest could take place, though, public security authorities moved in and arrested at least nine of the women organizing the action, accusing them of "picking quarrels and provoking trouble." While some were quickly released, five remained in custody and soon became known as the Feminist Five.

The Feminist Five case outraged onlookers, both within China and around the world. US politicians and diplomats, such as Hillary Clinton, John Kerry, and Samantha Power, issued calls for their release. Although not all Chinese supported the women's causes or their tactics (in a previous protest against domestic violence they had worn wedding dresses smeared with blood), many ordinary people also urged the government to release the Feminist Five. After five weeks of detention, authorities freed the women—although, like Ai Weiwei, they remain under government surveillance and risk re-arrest if they push the boundaries too far.[32]

The Feminist Five case is an example of how the space for protest has shrunk since Xi came to power. Gender equality and feminist causes are, at least officially, endorsed by the CCP, and in the past they have fallen into the safe zone of issues that could be publicly discussed. But the arrest of the Feminist Five signaled that the safe zone had disappeared.

What is the role of the Internet in political dissent?

It would be easy to imagine that the Chinese Internet is a hotbed of political dissent, particularly since the government sometimes seems preoccupied with silencing, often clumsily, discordant voices. But for many—perhaps even most—young Chinese, the Internet is simply an entertainment outlet: a place where they can chat with friends, make purchases, and play games late into the night (leading to a number of articles in the press about the dangers of Internet addiction). For a time, there were a few prominent outspoken bloggers, such as Ai Weiwei and the race car driver and writer Han Han (1982–); a far greater number of bloggers, though, were not interested in promoting political change. Yet Chinese who go online remain passionate about being able to express their opinions on topics that interest them and to follow stories that strike them as important, and as different platforms get censored their users seek out new online homes.[33]

Between 2009 and 2013, the place for sharing stories and opinions—and occasionally attracting censure from the authorities—was a Twitter-like microblogging platform called Weibo. In addition to sharing cat videos and photos of their dinners, like social-media users anywhere in the world, Chinese Weibo users also posted stories of corruption and official malfeasance, which censors often rushed to take down from the site before they could be picked up by others. Despite the rumored tens of thousands of censors the government employs, however, removing Weibo posts was much like playing a game of Whac-A-Mole: as soon as the content was deleted in one location, it popped up in another. And though censors could block particular terms on Weibo sites, users proved adept at finding innocuous homophones (using different written characters) to evade those blocks. For example, when a Weibo poster complained about his dislike of river crabs (*hexie*), savvy readers would understand that his real target was the Harmonious Society (*hexie shehui*) program that Hu Jintao made his signature effort while he was China's president.

For several years, Chinese Internet authorities allowed Weibo discussions to continue, while censoring any that appeared too threatening to either the government or social stability. Eventually Weibo proved a victim of its own success and growth. During the summer of 2013, the authorities cracked down on online dissent and rumor-mongering. They went after some of Weibo's most popular users, known as "Big Vs" due to their "verified" status (meaning they had been confirmed to be writing under their own names rather than pseudonyms), and in essence decapitated the platform.[34] Users fled en masse for a new online venue, known as Weixin (or WeChat outside China).

While Weibo posts were public, Weixin is designed for closed social networking—users organize themselves into groups and chat within those circles. Weixin, however, is not just Facebook to Weibo's Twitter. It is a powerful app through which users can also pay bills, order food or a shared ride, connect with business associates, and make purchases online. It has transformed how hundreds of millions of Chinese interact, shop, and navigate the world. Still, like any communications platform, Weixin is monitored by the Chinese government and always runs the risk of censure or shutdown if its users cross the shifting line of what's permissible to discuss online.

What does the digital divide mean in China?

It has become common to refer to a digital divide that separates those who use the Web from those who do not. The digital divide persists in most of the world, of course. Some people have their own laptops and fast Internet access, for example, whereas others can use the Internet only at a cybercafé, and still others have only occasional access to a computer with a slow connection.

In China, however, there is another level of distinction due to the government's sophisticated censorship mechanisms, which some refer to as "The Great Firewall of China" and others describe as the working of the "Net Nanny." These tools strive to make some sites inaccessible and to ensure that searches for sensitive terms yield either no results or only links that provide government-sanctioned information.

A search for the term "June 4th" will likely retrieve no results at all, for example, and a search for "Tiananmen" will deliver links to official sites devoted to the square but will not point the searcher to overseas sites containing student manifestos issued at Tiananmen in 1989. There are, however, ways to circumvent the Great Firewall and frustrate the Net Nanny. These involve proxy servers and VPNs (virtual private networks)—tools that, in a sense, make it seem as though a computer located in China is actually based somewhere else. This creates another divide among Internet users in China, separating those who are versed in employing such techniques from those who are not.

Still another divide, one that is less absolute, lies between what could be called critical and non-critical users of the Internet. There are those who do not question the nature of information provided online and whether it reinforces or challenges official viewpoints. There are also some readers and writers who access the mainland's government-controlled Web largely, though not exclusively, with an eye toward conveying or consuming alternative perspectives. They take pride in posting provocative comments that can stay online at least temporarily due to clever forms of wording, from using "river crab" to refer to "harmony" to using the Chinese terms for the imaginary date of "May 35th" to allude to June 4th.

Is the Great Firewall of China a unique structure?

The Chinese government's Internet policies can cause one to overstate the distinctiveness of the PRC. Contributing to a vision of uniqueness in this case is nomenclature. The term "Great Firewall of China" offers a nice rhetorical twist on the country's best-known landmark. And not only Western commentators use it. Many Chinese bloggers have had fun with the phrase as well—so much so that references to and images of "wall climbers" became very popular in Chinese cyberspace in 2009.[35] And yet what the Chinese government is doing vis-à-vis the Internet has plenty of foreign parallels.

In fact, many regimes limit the kinds of materials that can be accessed online within the territories they govern. The Iranian government is a case in point. Similarities between Chinese and Iranian bloggers had been noted before, but the analogies between how these countries controlled the Internet became particularly clear in June 2009. That month opened with Beijing officials trying to limit online discussion of the twentieth anniversary of the 1989 protests and ended with their counterparts in Tehran clamping down on social media, such as Twitter, and generally employing related strategies— though in a clumsier manner than the Chinese authorities—in a largely unsuccessful effort to curtail the spread of information about a popular movement.[36]

Non-authoritarian regimes also seek to control what goes online, limiting certain kinds of communications (often those deemed pornographic or with links to terrorism).[37] Some of the precise measures that the Chinese regime uses to limit the Internet are distinctive, but Beijing's leaders are not in a class all their own. The PRC is one of a variety of places (Singapore and Saudi Arabia, for example), in which a good deal of energy is spent trying to get Internet users to go to preferred sites and to steer clear of "harmful" modes of online behavior.[38]

Chinese Internet controls are also not absolute and do not move in only one direction. Sites that have been blocked occasionally get unblocked, and the list of search terms subject to censorship varies a great deal depending on current events and upcoming anniversaries. As major Chinese government events, such as the quinquennial party congresses, approach, Internet speeds (especially in Beijing, considered a sensitive location as it is the seat of government) slow to a crawl and VPN users find themselves unable to connect. Conversely, the government sometimes relaxes (though never releases) its grip on the Internet in certain places or at times when it feels pressured to do so by foreign attention being turned on the country, such as during the Beijing Olympics in 2008.[39]

Why was hosting its first Olympics such a big deal for China?

Large-scale anniversary spectacles, including the National Day parades held on October 1 every ten years, have long played important roles in the political life of the PRC. Recently, while continuing this tradition with such events as the big military-themed September 2015 parade held to mark the seventieth anniversary of World War II's end, the government has also hosted high-profile international gatherings, from summits to film festivals to large-scale sporting events, that bring people from around the world to China. The 2008 Beijing Summer Olympic Games were the biggest spectacle of this kind ever held in the PRC, and the government deemed them such a success that it immediately began lobbying to host its first Winter Olympics. (It succeeded, and the 2022 games will be held in the greater Beijing region.)

The government greeted with enthusiasm the news in 2001 that the Chinese bid for the 2008 games had been accepted. There was a great deal of popular excitement about the games, too, as many Chinese were well aware that the Olympics are the most attention-grabbing mega-event in the world, one that gives considerable prestige to the chosen host countries.

Not everyone was happy with the preparations necessary to stage the event. For example, the Olympics-related building boom required many long-term Beijing residents to relocate to less central districts. When residents felt that the compensation offered was appropriate and replacement accommodations represented an improvement, they made the move willingly. But some felt that the deals offered were too stingy or were distressed at having to abandon neighborhood ties and memory-filled haunts. Developers were often accused of bullying tactics and taking unfair advantage of official connections. Beijing also went to great lengths to upgrade its ground transportation system, expanding from two subway lines to six (there are now nineteen, and plans for more), and built a completely new state-of-the-art airport.

What does the handling of the Beijing Olympic Games say about today's China?

The elaborate preparations for the Beijing Games and other international events, including the 2010 Shanghai World Expo touted as an Economic Olympics, suggest that there is an unusual intensity to China's preoccupation with mega-events. But it has been common for countries that are rising rapidly in global hierarchies to start hosting both Olympics and World's Fair–like spectacles, as the United States did between 1876, the year of the Philadelphia Centennial Exhibition, the first World's Fair to be held in North America, and the early 1900s, when the country began playing host to the games.

The most important general point about World's Fairs (formerly the dominant international mega-events) and the Summer Olympics (the spectacle that currently holds that distinction, due partly to the rise of television and the way the games lend themselves to visual media coverage) is that they often have the effect of symbolically dividing countries into different categories, as much a measure of global status as economic development and military might. It is no mere coincidence that when World's Fairs were dominant, they were often staged in cities that were the capitals of major empires. Paris hosted four between 1855 and 1900, while London hosted two of the first three ever staged. Several of the first major International Exhibitions were held in the United States, when the country was rapidly industrializing, becoming much more urban, and beginning to assert itself forcefully on the global stage—as China is now.

China's dream to host both the Olympics and a World's Fair dates to the early 1900s (a 1902 science fiction story by a Chinese intellectual imagined an international exhibition in Shanghai in the then far-off year of 1962) as does the ambition to produce athletes who would win medals at the games. The significance of this last dream was intimately tied to a desire to shed the nation's global reputation as the "sick man of Asia" (a phrase that echoed the Ottoman Empire's tag, "sick man of Europe"). This vision of Chinese weakness, which followed the Qing defeats, first at the hands of Western powers and then Japan, was one that nationalists of all political stripes were eager to shed.

Both Mao and Chiang Kai-shek placed an emphasis on physical education in their early writings, and the public displays of stamina that the former exhibited later in life (such as his famous swims in the Yangzi River), are relevant here as well. The quest for Olympic glory, both in terms of medal winning and hosting rights, can thus be seen in part as an expression of China's desire to put behind it, once and for all, any lingering sense that it is enfeebled.

Is contemporary China utterly unique?

China's hybrid economic and political system defies easy categorization, and the PRC's post-Mao and (to an even greater extent) post-Tiananmen trajectory seems to have broken several basic rules of historical development. Never before has a process of industrialization and urbanization occurred so rapidly and on so vast a scale. This makes China's rise seem very different from the rapid growth that occurred in nearby Asian countries, such as Singapore.

In addition, no other country ruled by a communist party has ever overseen a period of runaway economic growth like China's. This sets the CCP apart not just from the state socialist regimes that fell from power late in the last century, but also from the main enduring ones, such as those of North Korea, Cuba, and Vietnam, none of which have achieved economic growth that comes close to matching China's.

There is, moreover, something special about the way that China confounds categorization along a capitalist/socialist axis. For example, many countries, including Scandinavian ones such as Sweden, can be aptly described as combining elements of capitalism and socialism. There are also many nations (including the United States) where the line between the governmental and private sectors can get very blurry, thanks in part to officials in one administration becoming consultants to industry as soon as they are out of power. Still, the borders between capitalist and socialist and bureaucratic and business sectors in today's China are especially tricky to draw.

This is because China's boom has been fueled by entrepreneurial activity and foreign investment, yet large state-run enterprises not only remain in operation but continue to be a major force within the overall economy—largely because the central government considers them as proverbially "too big to fail" and ensures that they don't. Moreover, many of the new "private" companies one hears about turn out to be run by the children of CCP leaders or others with strong links to the party.[40]

It is useful, up to a point, to think of China as a country of crony capitalism, a term that has been used to describe certain Latin American countries and India at specific points in their history. Even this phrase, though, does not seem to quite "scratch where it itches," in terms of accurately characterizing what is going on in the country now.[41]

It is also useful, again up to a point, to view China as under the control of leaders who engage in "adaptive authoritarianism."

This would place it in the category of other countries, such as Vladimir Putin's Russia, in which authoritarian figures make use of new media and take a pragmatic and often only vaguely ideological approach to staying in power.[42] We should not, however, regard the CCP's commitment to Marxism as a purely cynical one; from all outward appearances, Xi and his colleagues truly do believe in the importance of socialist theory for moving China forward.

In light of contradictory and confusing factors such as these, and given how difficult it is to place the PRC into any of the categories routinely used to categorize nations, it is easy to see why many have sought to characterize China by way of newly coined terms that emphasize its unusual aspects, such as "Market-Leninism" and "capitalism with Chinese characteristics" (a play upon official talk of "socialism with Chinese characteristics").[43] These terms have value, but it is a mistake to overstate China's exoticness. A precise mix of elements does make the PRC's trajectory sui generis, but many things going on there parallel those that have occurred or are occurring in other countries, including those without communist governments.

What does China have in common with other countries?

Many phenomena can be cited to illustrate the seductiveness, but also the problem, with highlighting China's distinctiveness. Consider, for example, the way China and India tend to be discussed together. The two countries are usually presented as a study in contrasts because only India has a federal system (which gives states great autonomy), and China does not hold national-level elections (while India is routinely described as the world's biggest democracy). The developmental paths of the "Dragon" and the "Elephant" are seen as very different.

There are many ways, however, in which the experiences of the two most populous countries in the world can be compared to highlight similarities, and thereby shed light on one another. The PRC, like India, took its modern form as a nation-state in the 1940s, and in the 1950s economic five-year plans were the order of the day in both countries. By the 1960s, Cold War visions of a clear communist/free world binary notwithstanding, Chinese and Indian leaders were each trying to find a place for their respective country that would keep it out of the shadow of both the United States and the Soviet Union. Then in the late 1970s, both sought to discover a developmental path that was unique and became fascinated by the Singapore model. Despite the enormous differences in scale between this city-state and China and India, Singapore was a polity that had suffered under imperialism and then, after independence, experienced an economic boom.

Developments in one country can be used to illuminate those in the other. The Chinese interest in using mega-events to show that the PRC is now a modern rather than a "backward" country, for example, has an Indian parallel. New Delhi hosted the 2010 Commonwealth Games, an Olympic-like spectacle preceded by an ambitious urban redevelopment drive that, while not as costly and over-the-top as that which preceded the Beijing Games, brought to mind the lead-up to the 2008 Olympic Opening Ceremonies. There was a great deal of hand-wringing in the Indian press at the time of China's Olympic success because Indians feared it would be difficult for their country to put on as polished a show. But this only underlines the ambitions within each country to use dramatic acts to shed the sense of backwardness they have carried since Western empires, and for a time Japan's, dominated the world.

China-India comparisons can also be useful for many other topics. For example, both countries have seen outbursts of inter-ethnic, religiously inflected communal violence over the years (in China, this is largely associated with Muslim residents of Xinjiang, while in India it is more geographically and ethnically diffuse).[44] Both countries are also dealing with the environmental consequences of economic development, chief among them cities with some of the world's worst air pollution.[45] It has recently become common for scholars and journalists to draw parallels between the strongman leadership of Xi Jinping and Indian Prime Minister Narendra Modi (the strongman group also includes Vladimir Putin, Donald Trump, and Japan's Shinzo Abe), but China–India comparisons go deeper than the actions of any two individual leaders.

Due to its distinctive history and the sheer size of its population, rivaled only by that of India, China is in some ways unique. It has also followed a political path that, in certain regards, is unlike that of any other nation. However, to make sense of the country's current situation, we need to balance consideration of what sets it apart from and what makes it like other nations. And one country that Americans should realize has many things in common with today's China, as we will see in chapter 5, is their own.

5

US–CHINA
MISUNDERSTANDINGS

*What is the most common thing Americans get wrong
about China?*

The preceding chapters have drawn attention to some important
sources of US misunderstanding of Chinese realities. Discussion
of the One-Child Policy, for example, noted a tendency for
Americans to treat unintended side-effects of a Chinese government policy as part of the policy itself. Additionally, reactions
to the violence of 1989 showed how recent historical events are
sometimes misconstrued. Finally, Americans are often inclined—
partly as a result of pronouncements coming out of and pageants
staged in Beijing—to accept the notion of an enduring and relatively unchanged five-thousand-year-old Chinese civilization.

The most deeply rooted and persistent US misconception
about China involves its diversity. Americans think of China
as populated by people who are all pretty much alike—or, at
least, can be neatly divided into one large group and a smaller
number of "others." We have seen examples of this already,
such as in the idea that in political terms China has only
"loyalists" and "dissidents." There are, however, many other
realms in which either this homogeneity or false dichotomy
makes an appearance.

Why is China's diversity overlooked?

The view of China as a homogeneous land goes back hundreds of years. Between Marco Polo's day—the late thirteenth century—and World War II, Westerners generally depicted China as a land of menacing hordes of faceless and essentially interchangeable people hostile to foreigners. Periodically there emerged a more positive variant of this motif, such as in the film *The Good Earth*, based on Nobel Prize-winning US writer Pearl Buck's 1931 novel of the same title. The popular 1937 movie portrays China as composed of villages of poor and hardworking (if largely interchangeable) families.[1]

Notions of Chinese homogeneity gained new force during the first decades of the Cold War era, when the wartime image of Japan as a militaristic land led by madmen was simply transposed to China, while the Japanese, now allies of the United States, were portrayed as industrious and peaceful. Thanks to the way the Western press covered the Korean War and then the Cultural Revolution, the word "China" began to conjure in many Western minds a picture of lookalike and blindly obedient men and women in blue Mao suits. This vision of conformity was rooted in part in actual efforts by the Chinese government to create a country where everyone had much in common, but those efforts were given a decidedly negative spin internationally—a perspective that showed through in book titles such as the 1961 *Mao Tse-tung: Emperor of the Blue Ants*.

This misconception has been challenged in recent decades by news coverage that stresses differences within China. Unfortunately, such reportage often still manages to misconstrue Chinese society by presenting its citizens as falling into just two groups (e.g., dissidents and loyalists) or drawing simplistic contrasts between life in the city and countryside. Still, the "Empire of the Blue Ants" notion has a long half-life, as was evidenced in 1999, when students took to the streets to express their outrage at NATO bombs hitting the PRC embassy in Belgrade. Some Western commentators called this a new form of Boxerism, and one US magazine likened the protesters to the Borg of the Star Trek universe, an entity made up of drones without the capacity for independent thought.[2]

In reality, the participants in the demonstrations took part for varied reasons and conveyed their anger via unapproved as well as approved means. Some called for a boycott of US goods, though official spokesmen insisted there should be no boycotts. Others sometimes followed—although not unconditionally—government efforts to turn the movement into one that served CCP goals. The regime, far from feeling comfortable with the alleged manipulability of the students, moved quickly to get the youths off the streets and back into classrooms, lest they begin to protest issues relating to national authorities' failings in addition to those of NATO.[3]

How does ethnicity contribute to the myth of homogeneity?

One reason that Americans tend to overlook diversity within China is that ethnicity and race loom large in US discussions of heterogeneity and homogeneity, while the Chinese government asserts that its country is 90 percent Han.

China can accurately be described as somewhat less heterogeneous than other large countries. It has neither the dizzying religious diversity of India nor the linguistic complexity of Indonesia. It does not have as many inhabitants whose parents, grandparents, or great-grandparents were born in distant lands as the United States does. But there is a world of difference between saying the PRC is *somewhat less heterogeneous* than other countries and suggesting that its people are mostly *basically the same*.

And when it comes to ethnicity, the assumption of relative homogeneity misleads. Even if one accepts the 90 percent Han number—which is a problematic one, as there is always something vexing about such categories—there are many within this capacious majority catchall group who speak mutually unintelligible dialects and have radically dissimilar customs.[4] To cite just one illustration, the Hakka, or "guest people" (*Kejia*), scattered around China are considered Han but have many characteristics that, in another context, might easily lead observers to categorize them as ethnically distinct. Among many other things, the Hakka never embraced any form of foot-binding, a practice that was itself far less uniform than outsiders have often suggested. There are many historical cases of conflicts that pit Hakka against non-Hakka and might be described as inter-ethnic, such as the Taiping Uprising (Hong Xiuquan was a Hakka), which began with an inter-ethnic dimension and later took on a Han-versus-Manchu element.[5]

How important are regional divides?

Further complicating the issue is the fact that people from various Chinese regions often view one another the way, for example, Belgians typically regard the French and vice versa. Residents of Beijing view their counterparts in Shanghai as inferior—and Shanghai residents return the favor. The terminology that some Han urbanites use for Han migrants from the countryside, in which the former imply or state that the latter are less than fully human, resembles terms Americans describe as racist when skin color is involved.[6] The government itself has encouraged such discourse with its own discussions of the *suzhi*, or "quality," of Chinese citizens. *Suzhi* broadly encompasses education, manners, and morality, with a hint of genetics thrown in as well. It is mostly linked in the common imagination with an urban-rural divide: middle-class urbanites pride themselves on their high *suzhi*, while denigrating the rural migrants who perform low-skilled service work in the city as being of low *suzhi*.[7] Location and point of origin are thus a crucial source of diversity in the PRC today, as is *when* rather than *where* one was born.

How important are age divides in China?

During the 1960s, Americans began speaking of a generation gap between children born after World War II and their parents, due to clashes over political opinions and cultural tastes. In more recent decades, developing countries have also seen generation gaps emerge, often related to younger people's desires for urban, globalized lifestyles while their parents are more comfortable with traditional practices. These differences exist in China, and the speed with which the country has changed in the past several decades makes the generation gap in the PRC a chasm of unusual size.

China's population has been aging: the 2010 census counted PRC citizens age sixty and older as 9 percent of the population, up two percentage points from the 2000 census. While China's youth population was much larger—in 2010 about 17 percent of Chinese were age fifteen or younger—its size had actually declined from the prior decade, when 23 percent were in the 0–14 age range.[8] Still, for a large proportion of Chinese, Mao has always been dead, and the Berlin Wall has always been rubble. Switching from political to social issues, younger generations have only known a country marked by a large divide separating those who have benefited most from the reforms and those who have been left behind by them. Those between forty-five and seventy have a memory of more egalitarian times, and those older than that may see the current disparities between "haves" and "have nots" as a return of sorts to an economic division they knew in their childhoods.

In cultural terms, those in their early thirties today will likely be the last generation to remember when the main phones were still shared by work units and neighborhoods and the main urban vehicles were still bikes and buses. And yet, those only a decade younger have likely always had mobile phones and now think nothing of using them to hail a ride-sharing car or pay a restaurant tab. Chinese aged forty and over have experienced much larger cultural shifts, not once but several times in their lives, from the years of the Cultural Revolution to Deng's economic reforms to the globalization of the 1990s.

These generation gaps influence an enormous number of things, from attitudes toward the pace of modern life (unsettling to some and bracing to others) to views of China's place in the world. And they affect phenomena that are presented as transcendent.

Consider, for example, the supposedly timeless Chinese attachment to Confucian values, such as social harmony. The oldest residents of the PRC—now in their eighties at least—can remember a time when China was governed by the Nationalist regime, which venerated Confucius and made much of the need to follow his moral dictates. For Chinese born between the mid- to late 1940s and the early 1960s, by contrast, the current celebration of Confucius and his ideas may seem a bit odd, since they may remember mass campaigns to criticize all vestiges of Confucian thought. But for Chinese born since the 1980s and unfamiliar with this history (it is ignored or glossed over in schoolbooks, and their parents sometimes prefer not to talk about it), there has been nothing remarkable about first Hu Jintao and now Xi Jinping embracing Confucius.

Is China a Big Brother state?

Some US misconceptions about the PRC can be tied to a tendency to think of all countries run by communist party regimes as Big Brother states. When the Soviet Union existed, it was thought to be the place where George Orwell's *1984* had come to life. Since the fall of the USSR, China has often been cast in that same role. Now, even though many commentators argue that North Korea fits the bill most neatly, the adjective "Orwellian" is still often applied to China.

It might be more useful to look to *Brave New World*, the classic 1932 novel by Aldous Huxley (who was among Orwell's teachers at Eton).[9] Both *1984* and *Brave New World* often show up together on high-school reading lists, and each is set in a future world where individual freedoms are greatly limited. They do, however, present contrasting visions of authoritarianism. Orwell emphasizes the role of fear in keeping people in line, while Huxley shows how needs and desires are created, manipulated, and satisfied.

The use of *1984* and *Brave New World* as contrasting dystopian visions goes back at least as far as October 1949—the very month that the PRC was established. In a letter to his former student, Huxley noted that *1984* was a "profoundly important" book but that he thought that the kind of "boot-on-the-face" authoritarian regime it described would soon be a thing of the past. In the future, he suspected, ruling oligarchies would find "less arduous" methods for satisfying their "lust" for power. These rulers would stay in control via the softer means he had sketched out in *Brave New World*, which stresses the depoliticizing effect of keeping people apart and providing them with distracting forms of activity and entertainment.[10]

Here, again, the Internet provides a useful way of seeing how this thorny issue relates to China. In this case, the question is whether Orwell or Huxley provides the better guide to making sense of Chinese political and cultural shifts.

The Chinese government's efforts to monitor and control citizens' use of the Internet are routinely described as Orwellian.[11] Appropriate as the term is to some extent, some have pointed out that the Internet is at least as much *Brave New World* as *1984*, given that most Chinese who go online ignore government attempts to censor content so long as they can access entertainment and chat with their friends.[12]

When bringing the contrast between Orwell's "hard" and Huxley's "soft" visions of authoritarianism into discussions of China, temporal issues are worth considering. The Chinese political system has never been static; the strategies that the state turns to are always shifting. The pattern has often been for alternating periods of what observers refer to as "tightening" and "loosening." This was clearest during the Mao years, when periods of intense mobilization via mass campaigns were followed by periods of relative quiescence. There was also a tightening in the immediate wake of the 1986–1987 student protests, followed by a loosening in 1988. In recent years, the interplay between tightening and loosening has been more subtle—especially regarding the latter, so much so that it's possible the old pattern has been broken. For example, journalists and NGOs were given a bit more freedom between around 2001 and the beginning of 2008. Then there was a shift toward tightening during the following year, and then, without any dramatic loosening, a ratcheting up of controls in early 2011, late 2012, and most dramatically of all during the lead-up to the Nineteenth Party Congress midway through 2017. In each instance, the space for activism and open discussion of sensitive issues has shrunk dramatically, giving more of a *1984* cast to life in the PRC.

The PRC went through what we would call an Orwellian moment between 1989 and 1992, which began with the killing of protesters, a "2 + 2 = 5" style denial that state violence had occurred, and the detention of many alleged "black hands" (as noted, a CCP term for troublemakers). The PRC had entered a more Huxleyan stretch by the mid-1990s, for by that point—though it continued to deny that there had been a massacre in 1989—the state was focusing largely on fostering a consumer revolution that it hoped would achieve a kind of mass depoliticization. The government was occupied, to use the *Brave New World* term for a powerful soporific drug, with producing "Soma-like" effects.

Though there has been an ebbing and flowing of "hard" and "soft" forms of authoritarianism over time, geographic and ethnic dimensions also come into play. In areas with significantly large and periodically restive non-Han populations, such as Xinjiang and Tibet, the modes of control tend to remain much more *1984*, even when the country as a whole is in a *Brave New World* mode. Conversely, in booming east coast cities such as Shanghai, with their cultures of distraction epitomized by glittering department stores and massive video screens, Huxley tends to be the better guide. And, so far, the former colonies of Hong Kong and Macao have never, since becoming part of the PRC in the late 1990s, been subjected fully to *1984*-like suppression, although as political unrest has grown in Hong Kong, Beijing has taken a more assertive hand, moving, for example, to limit freedom of the press. The local police have also grown more prone to use "boot-on-the-face" techniques against protesters, including the spraying of tear gas near the start of the Umbrella Movement in September 2014 (about which more below).

What is the most common thing Chinese get wrong about the United States?

Simply put, the biggest Chinese misunderstanding of the United States is a failure to appreciate how the media works. At the root of this problem, which produces many other misunderstandings, is the belief that the US media system as a whole—spanning venues from the *New York Times* to CNN to Fox News—is unwaveringly biased against the PRC. Three things contribute to the staying power of this notion. Understanding what these factors are and how they work together to create a deeply rooted sense of unfairness on the part of the Chinese tells us something important that all foreigners, not just Americans, need to know about China.

One contributing factor is that the Western press is predisposed, in a way that media in the PRC are not, to emphasize bad news. It is an axiom of Western journalism in general that "if it bleeds, it leads." That is, stories of tragedy and hardship sell more papers (and attract more viewers, whether of websites or of television screens) than do tales of happiness—or, even worse, tales of simple contentment. The PRC state media, however, have long focused to an overwhelming degree on positive developments, at least when discussing China (higher living standards, less hunger, faster trains, etc.). Recently, tabloids, blogs, and Weibo/Weixin posts that focus on more downbeat tales of woe have become both more common and more popular, but in the official media, good news about domestic issues remains the norm. Hence, even if the Western press treats the PRC like any other country, the perception of many Chinese used to rosier approaches to journalism would be that their country was being treated in an unusually harsh way, not in a routine fashion.

A second contributing factor is that it is not common in contemporary Chinese media to showcase contrasting views on a topic. Many Chinese assume (usually correctly) that a commentary that appears in a major Beijing or Shanghai newspaper reflects the opinion of its publishers, and by extension the government. Moreover, state media directives often lead newspapers across the country to run virtually identical coverage of major events, even down to the photos used on the front page.[13] By contrast, the *New York Times* may run two opinion pieces on a subject by people who disagree, plus an editorial of its own that stakes out a third position. If any one of the three pieces in question attacks China, however, and people begin to talk about it and share a translation online, many Chinese readers will easily assume that this represents the view of the *Times*.

A third contributing factor is that there are simply some issues on which standard Chinese and standard US assumptions diverge so greatly that a perception of bias is almost guaranteed to be generated or reinforced—no matter how "fairly" the US media handle a PRC story. One way to illustrate this is via the case of a March 2008 conflict in Tibet, which reveals clearly how entering a story from radically different perspectives can lead to two sides talking past rather than to one another.

How do US and Chinese views on Tibet differ?

For many Americans, the starting point for thinking about Tibet has tended to be that the Tibetans are a peace-loving and oppressed people, who have throughout most of their history been self-governing. Their leader in exile, the Dalai Lama, is regarded as an enlightened man, so committed to nonviolence that he won a Nobel Peace Prize.

In the United States, many view the Dalai Lama as someone who has shown great restraint by agitating only for greater cultural autonomy and religious freedom for Tibetans within the PRC, rather than calling for the establishment of an independent state. The vision of the Tibetan struggle as a defense of religious freedom by a people who are under the thumb of a foreign power, while influential in many parts of the West (and other places), takes on special force in the United States because of its own specific history and nationalist mythology. The US view casts the Tibetans in a role not unlike that played by the New England colonists who fought against the British Empire, a fight that looms large in the US patriotic imagination.

The starting point for many citizens of the PRC is radically different. They assume—based on school history lessons and state propaganda in the media—that Tibet has long been part of China and that the traditions of the region are backward and feudal. The evidence for this is, in part, a tendency to express fanatic loyalty to each new Dalai Lama, a man who is ascribed a role that is part monarch and part pope and considered a reincarnation of his predecessor. This leads to a sense that Tibetans should be grateful to Beijing for having modernized cities such as Lhasa, raised the status of Tibetan women through laws based on principles of gender equality, and introduced scientific practices to a superstitious land. Some Han Chinese also think that ethnic Tibetans should be grateful for having received various kinds of special treatment from the state, such as being able to benefit from university admissions policies that favor members of ethnic minority groups.

The gulf between the two starting points just described is so vast that those on opposite sides of it are predisposed to view the other's accounts of any event involving Tibet as completely off base. While many in the United States would find it natural to compare Tibetans who take to the streets to the heroic colonists of 1776, many in the PRC would view these same actors more like an average American would participants in a rally calling for Hawaii to be returned to the descendants of the last king of those islands. In such a context, every account of a conflict pitting Tibetan and non-Tibetan residents of Tibet and nearby regions against one another, right down to the choice of words used to describe clashes and individuals, is bound to be contentious. What many Westerners would normally dub a demonstration, for example, many non-Tibetans in the PRC call a riot. The exiled Dalai Lama, whom many Westerners find natural to see referred to as a spiritual leader and Nobel laureate, many non-Tibetans in the PRC will find natural to see referred to as a "wolf in monk's clothing," a "splittist," and so on.

Even careful and nuanced foreign reporting on Tibet can end up being interpreted by some Chinese as biased. It is also very difficult for foreign reporters to access Tibet in the first place, as the Chinese government virtually bans them from the region rather than risk what it expects to be negative media coverage. For example, the most thoughtful US journalists did sometimes use terms such as "riot" to refer to the outbursts of violence in March 2008. The term was objectively correct, given that there were times when ethnic Tibetan youths attacked local Han Chinese and members of the Hui minority group, who are Muslims. But this was still seen by some in the PRC as biased reporting, since the authors in question stopped short of blaming the Dalai Lama for the violence, as the official Chinese media did.

Less nuanced reporting, meanwhile, engendered a much stronger sense of unfairness within China. When CNN showed an image of police in Nepal engaging in violence and misidentified the shot as one of Chinese police beating up Tibetans, bloggers throughout the PRC wrote furious posts attacking the Atlanta-based network, an "anti-CNN" website was launched, and "Don't Be Like CNN" t-shirts sold in Shanghai. What might have been simple carelessness was immediately treated by many as just the latest indication of a deep-seated prejudice.

6

THE FUTURE

Is China bent on world domination?

Although Americans perceived the Soviet Union as posing the greatest Cold War-era military challenge, they also periodically feared a "China threat" during those decades. Since the days of Mao, the PRC's penchant for staging parades showing off its military hardware has made foreigners wary of the country's perceived aggressiveness.

This wariness builds upon anxieties that go back much further than Mao's day—and have an equally long history of tending to be overblown. While the Boxers never ventured outside of North China nor showed any interest in doing so, Kaiser Wilhelm treated them as the vanguard of a "Yellow Peril" poised to destroy the West. And he was not alone. Mark Twain defended the Boxers (even saying he would have joined the group if he had been born Chinese) and insisted that they were just trying to protect their own villages from foreign encroachment in a manner Americans should respect, yet some of his compatriots embraced the apocalyptic view of the German leader. One US magazine described the Boxers as constituting the greatest Asian threat to the West and Christendom since Genghis Khan's Mongol forces had swept into Europe in the thirteenth century. Newspapers on both sides of the Atlantic ran editorial cartoons that stoked Yellow Peril paranoia, including one that showed a fiendish-looking Boxer holding a bloody knife in his teeth and gripping a globe in his hands, implying that his group was bent on world domination.

The Yellow Peril myth continued throughout the first decades of the twentieth century, albeit sometimes with Japan rather than China represented as the aggressor. It spread in popular culture via books and movies, such as those featuring the diabolically cunning, Western-hating arch-villain Fu Manchu. After World War II ended and the Communists gained control of China, the notion of a Yellow Peril threatening the West morphed into visions of a Red Menace. This idea gained purchase in the early 1960s, when China produced its first atom bomb. Coming at a time when anti-imperialist rhetoric ran high in the PRC, this was a frightening development to the United States and the Soviet Union, both of which Mao was denouncing vociferously—the former for its capitalism and support of Taiwan, the latter for its "revisionist" abandonment of Marxism.

The US Department of Defense even produced a film, *Red Chinese Battle Plan*, in the 1960s that presented Beijing as intent upon global control. Updating imagery used in 1940s propaganda films that had represented China as one of the victims of Japanese plans for world domination, the film now depicted the PRC as seeking to first gain control of Africa and Latin America and then moving to take over the United States.

Getting the bomb was unquestionably important to China, but we now know that in the 1960s the PRC was so beset by internal problems and border disputes with neighboring countries, such as the Soviet Union and India, that there was no real likelihood of its military threatening any distant land. China did seek allies in the nonaligned states of the developing world, presenting itself as an alternative to the United States and the Soviet Union. Still, fears of a Red Menace were no more rooted in reality than were fears of the Yellow Peril.

Proxy wars between the United States and communist countries did occur between the 1950s and 1970s. And there were times when cross-strait skirmishes between the Communists of Beijing and the Nationalists of Taipei, each of whom claimed to be the rightful ruler of all of China, could have escalated into a direct war between the PRC and the United States. But there was no serious Chinese plan for world domination then.

And there is none now. China has begun restructuring its military—both hardware and personnel—to emphasize technology and sophistication, rather than sheer size and brute force, its past markers of strength. It is also shifting focus from the PLA ground force to its naval and air force branches, which play a larger role in securing the PRC's regional interests in Asia.[1] This is and should be a source of concern to its immediate neighbors, especially countries with which it has ongoing border disputes, such as India and Russia, and countries, including Vietnam and Japan, that claim sovereignty over islands that Beijing insists are part of China.

The transformation of the PLA is not, however, just about having the ability to project force abroad. The regime still thinks of itself as needing to ensure that China is not attacked (recent US construction of a missile-defense system in South Korea is among the things keeping this sense of the need for a strong defense alive, even though Washington's rationale for placing those weapons there is to combat potential North Korean aggression).

And, at least as significantly, the PRC also sees having a powerful military as crucial for maintaining control at home. It was the PLA, not a civilian police force, that carried out the June 4th crackdown, after all, and the government relies upon its army to deal with unrest in places such as Tibet and Xinjiang. The showcasing of military hardware during parades, such as a lavish one held in 2015 to mark the seventieth anniversary of World War II's conclusion, can be seen as being as much an effort to remind domestic audiences of the sophistication of the weaponry of the state as an effort to make an impact on foreign observers. And although Beijing has not yet used military force to quell protests in Hong Kong, that is an ever-present possibility that both demonstrators and observers discuss each time a major protest takes place.

What is the future of relations between Beijing and Hong Kong?

When Great Britain handed over control of Hong Kong to Beijing on July 1, 1997, the former colony became a Special Administrative Region (SAR) of the PRC, governed under a principle termed "one country, two systems." This meant that although part of China, Hong Kong would be governed differently. For example, its residents would retain some of the rights and privileges they had enjoyed under British rule, including a high degree of freedom of expression. The territory would also keep its independent judiciary. A new mini-constitution called the Basic Law, which spelled out the nature of Hong Kong's "high degree of autonomy," was put into place. Both sides agreed that this arrangement would govern the relationship for fifty years—until 2047—at which point Hong Kong would be fully integrated into the PRC.

By the early 2010s, however, Beijing was displaying impatience with the sense of independence Hong Kongers continued to exhibit. Many things were possible in Hong Kong that were grounds for arrest only miles away: for example, the city staged a massive public vigil in memory of the 1989 victims every year on the anniversary of June 4th; authors published books on sensitive topics, including the allegedly shady backgrounds of some Chinese leaders; and protests spilled into the streets when citizens disagreed with the actions of their elected officials.

In 2012, the Chinese leadership made its first major attempt to more forcibly bring Hong Kong into the fold, announcing that the SAR's schools would implement a version of the patriotic education curriculum used on the mainland. Rather than passively accept this move, as Beijing probably expected they would, the citizens of Hong Kong staged large-scale protests against the proposed curriculum. Taking to the streets, they denounced patriotic education as brainwashing and contrary to the values of free and independent thinking that the city continued to hold. After several weeks of protest, the government backed down, but tensions between Hong Kong and the mainland continued to simmer.[2]

The 2012 protests were notable for drawing in many teenagers and young college graduates who were born around the time of the 1997 handover and had only known Hong Kong as part of the PRC, albeit a "special" part. These millennials were not only angry about the threat to Hong Kong's autonomy, they also found economic and employment conditions in the SAR frustrating: high-paying white-collar jobs were hard to find, and housing costs had skyrocketed so much (in part due to an influx of mainlanders) that few could afford to move out of their parents' apartments.

The situation boiled over again in September 2014, in a widespread protest movement originally known as Occupy Central and then called the Umbrella Movement. The catalyst for these protests came when officials in Beijing attempted to revise the criteria for the 2017 election of Hong Kong's chief executive in a way that would guarantee that only pre-screened pro-PRC candidates could run (and the same standards would also apply to the 2016 Legislative Council elections). Protesters—again, a great number of them millennials—initiated a sit-in outside the government headquarters in the city's Central district. Within days, the crowds had grown to fill the streets of both Central and the neighboring Admiralty district and brought the normally bustling area to a standstill. Another protest zone emerged in the vibrant Mong Kok neighborhood, on the other side of Victoria Harbour. Police attempted to drive back demonstrators in the Admiralty district by spraying them with tear gas; protesters protected their eyes by holding opened umbrellas in front of their faces, thus giving the movement its emblem.

Given the prominence of student activists in the Umbrella Movement, many people compared it to the 1989 Tiananmen protests—and some predicted that it would come to a similarly violent end. But while the police did use tear gas, and members of Hong Kong's underworld (allegedly hired by the government) assaulted protesters, no troops or tanks moved in to clear the city's streets. And although many of the movement's leaders were arrested (some multiple times) during the occupation of major thoroughfares in Central and other districts, they had access to lawyers and were released on bail, or were let go when judges declared that legal procedures had not been carried out correctly—all things that demonstrated how Hong Kong's rule of law remained in place.

The Umbrella Movement protests continued for more than two months before the demonstrators withdrew in mid-December, the occupation of Central fizzling out as the weeks passed and the government showed no willingness to compromise on its position. The protesters did not achieve their goal of striking down the proposed election rules (which have indeed been put into place).

The antagonism between Beijing and Hong Kong has only increased in the years since the protests, as the PRC government expands its influence in the SAR and Hong Kongers fight back. For example, in the fall of 2016 two young politicians who ran for and won election to the Legislative Council found themselves unseated by Beijing after they inserted anti-PRC language when taking their oaths of office. The city's once-vibrant publishing and media spheres have cooled off due to censorship. On several occasions, PRC security officials have also taken the unprecedented step of going into Hong Kong to detain people there, then bringing them back across the border. In the summer of 2017, three leaders of the Umbrella Movement, including Joshua Wong (the best-known Hong Kong student activist), who had originally been sentenced to community service for 2014 civil disobedience actions, were given prison terms after the local authorities—presumably under pressure from Beijing—complained that their original punishment had been too soft. All of these moves have caused great worry among those Hong Kongers who do not want to see their home be fully absorbed into the PRC. While resistance goes on, the clock on the fifty-year Basic Law also continues to tick down.

What is the likely future of PRC–Taiwan relations?

The relationship between Beijing and Taipei goes through occasional periods of warming, as well as periods of friction. In part, these periods are linked to which party is in power on Taiwan, and, ironically, relations tend to be freest of friction when the *Nationalist* Party, the CCP's pre-1949 arch-rival, is in control of Taiwan's government. For example, Nationalist president Ma Ying-jeou, who served from 2008 to 2016, favored improved ties with Beijing and even met with Xi Jinping at a 2015 summit in Singapore. Current president Tsai Ing-wen, on the other hand, who is from the Democratic Progressive Party (DPP), opposes PRC influence in Taiwan, and Beijing has taken steps in response to this, including discouraging its citizens from vacationing on the island. Regardless of these small shifts, on the whole the relationship has largely settled into a long-term "agree to disagree" stalemate, which is unlikely to change anytime soon, despite much rhetoric to the contrary from Beijing.

In previous decades, especially in the 1950s, some sort of armed conflict between the PRC and Taiwan appeared very possible. Many factors, however, now make it extremely unlikely that the PRC will use military force to try to achieve the long-held goal of reunification. The CCP still clings to the idea that there is only "one China," a notion that the separation of Taiwan from the mainland is a temporary aberration rather than a permanent state of affairs (something that Chiang Kai-shek also insisted on in his lifetime, due to his hope that someday he would regain control of the territory he lost), but it is hard to see how it would end up acting on it. The possibility of war cannot be discounted completely. There is always the chance that, if the CCP felt that it was in danger of falling, it might make a desperate bid at shoring up popular support by taking a dramatic course of action (such as by invading Taiwan) that it hoped would appeal to extreme nationalist sentiment.

There is very little likelihood of this happening, for several reasons. First, money and people move across the straits regularly and in ways that benefit both countries. In the 1990s, many Taiwanese companies relocated their manufacturing facilities to mainland China, where labor costs were lower; today, there are over seventy thousand Taiwanese firms with operations in the PRC.[3] After decades during which there were no direct flights between the PRC and Taiwan, there are now hundreds every week, and although Beijing still monitors and controls the movement of PRC citizens to Taiwan, it is no longer unusual to choose the island as a vacation destination. Mainland students study in Taiwan, and vice versa; and every year, more than ten thousand women from the PRC marry Taiwanese men.[4] Disentangling these many connections would be difficult.

Second, the resistance that Beijing has encountered in its attempts to consolidate control over Hong Kong in the past several years would likely make PRC leaders wary of taking on another potentially troublesome entity. Like Hong Kongers, Taiwanese citizens have grown to expect democracy and freedom of expression (although these were only implemented after the lifting of martial law on the island in 1987) and will not hesitate to protest if they perceive their rights have been curtailed. In the spring of 2014, students angry with a Taiwan–PRC trade agreement that they felt was too favorable to the mainland stormed the main parliamentary chamber in Taipei, which they occupied for twenty-four days. This "Sunflower Movement" illustrates how deeply many young Taiwanese oppose control by Beijing.[5] Unlike previous generations, who remembered life on the mainland, today's youth identify more strongly with a local Taiwan identity and would almost certainly fight any real attempt at reunification.

At the present time, PRC leaders appear willing to accept the relationship as it has developed—with the occasional dip or spike in response to events that they oppose or favor—and likely consider reunification more trouble than it's worth. For symbolic purposes, however, they refuse to give up on One China, and insist that the United States and other countries accept this fiction as a basis for diplomatic relations. A clear reminder of just how seriously Beijing continues to take this idea came at the start of Donald J. Trump's presidency. Just before taking office, Trump stated in a television interview that the One China policy should be up for negotiation, suggesting that as president he would only accept it if Beijing made concessions on other issues. By the end of his first post-inauguration phone conversation with Xi Jinping, though, both sides had reaffirmed that the One China principle would continue to serve as a basis for PRC–US diplomacy.

Will China become the world's dominant economic power?

There are good reasons to think that the United States will still be the world's dominant economic power for some time to come. It is a sign of just how much the PRC and its place in the world have changed in recent times, though, that such questions as this seem reasonable. Fifty years ago—indeed, even thirty years ago—when people speculated about China's future, this just was not a consideration.

In the late 1950s, Mao had boasted that the utopian Great Leap Forward would allow the country to catch up with the West quickly in metrics of development, such as amounts of steel produced. Very few people outside of the country, though, took these assertions seriously.

By the early 1960s, with the Great Leap clearly a failure, it would have seemed nothing short of ridiculous to consider that, in a mere half century, the PRC could move to the top ranks of economic powers. Had outsiders known the full extent of the horrific famine underway, they would have been even more dismissive of China's prospects. The most that was expected was that it would go from a fairly poor developing country to an only somewhat impoverished one. In contrast to today, when the PRC sometimes exports food to famine-stricken countries, the question then was whether China would be able to feed its own population.

Today only the United States stands higher in terms of gross domestic product. The long series of years of high—even double-digit—growth rates that China experienced just before and after the turn of the millennium changed it from a poor country to one that, while not rich (per capita income is still far behind that of developed countries), has enough wealth to help other countries when they are hit by disasters.

China's economy has slowed down since 2010, and double-digit growth rates now look to be a thing of the past; the leadership is instead focused on creating a "moderately prosperous society." Still, it is now likely that before another fifty years have passed the PRC and United States will run neck-and-neck on most measures of economic strength. It remains unlikely that China will surge far ahead of the United States as an economic power in the foreseeable future when measured in GDP, though likely that it will edge past it. It is much more unlikely that China will by that point have a population as well off in terms of per capita income, as by that metric the PRC is still a fairly poor country, just not nearly as poor as it was two or three decades ago.

How will urbanization shape China's future?

The question of China's world economic domination revolves in part around the pace of the PRC's transformation from a rural to an urban society, from a land of villages to a land of megacities. China circa 1960 was a country that seemed very likely to remain largely rural forever. This is because the CCP had developed rigid and elaborate social-welfare and social-control mechanisms to keep the rural-to-urban movement of people in check. Such movement had been common between the late 1800s and 1940s, when the population of cities such as Shanghai swelled into the millions, and it is happening again. Over 275 million internal migrants have headed into Chinese cities seeking work,[6] making China the site of the largest voluntary migration in the history of the world.[7]

The main obstacle to villagers relocating to cities during the Mao years was the *hukou,* or household registration system, which tied state-provided benefits, such as rations, healthcare, and education, to the locale in which one was born. Only in rare instances did individuals receive permission to move, except for betrothed women, who often switched households when they married. Those born into farming families had no choice but to work the land throughout their lives and have children who remained in their village.

This is no longer the case. The *hukou* system had begun to relax by 1990, thanks to the reforms implemented by Deng Xiaoping and his erstwhile protégé Zhao Ziyang, and villagers found it easier than before to go to cities for seasonal work and sometimes stay there long-term. Subsequent rounds of *hukou* reform—though not a complete dismantling of the system—have enabled even more urban migration. In early 2012, the Chinese government announced that the country's urban population exceeded its rural one for the first time in history.

There are limits to this migration, most notably regulations that keep migrant children out of public schools in those cities the government designates as first-tier (such as Beijing and Shanghai). The children's parents face a difficult choice: either enroll them in a lower-quality school for migrant children in the city, or leave the youngsters in the village with their grandparents to attend school there. Millions of parents have chosen the latter option, resulting in a population of "left-behind children" estimated at more than sixty million.[8] Migrant workers in first-tier cities also face limitations on access to other social services, such as healthcare, and no matter how long they live in the cities where they work, most will never become official urban residents.

Employment-driven migration, however, is not the only reason China is becoming a country of cities. The government is actively promoting urbanization below the first tier, creating hundreds of third- and fourth-tier cities, which officials hope will become sites of efficiency, innovation, consumption—and profit. Local governments requisition farmland surrounding existing small urban centers, then turn around and sell that land to developers, netting enormous sums. The former farmers are transformed into urban residents—though this exchange does not always proceed without incident.[9]

The 1990 census reported that China already had dozens of urban centers with more than one million residents. Today, there are at least one hundred and sixty cities with populations of a million or more, and eight of those are megacities with ten million-plus residents. Some of these cities, such as Shenzhen— a southern metropolis that was among the first special economic zones in which joint-venture enterprises that brought Chinese and foreign investors together are governed by looser rules than state-run companies—had been mere clusters of villages and towns just a decade or so earlier.

Is China likely to become a democracy?

In the years immediately following June 4th, some Western observers wondered if a sequel to the Tiananmen protests or a Chinese counterpart to the Polish Solidarity struggle would lead to China's democratization. Later in the 1990s, those hoping for a dramatic shift in China's political system put their faith in other forces. Some bet on the Internet: both conservative pundit George Will and former President Bill Clinton, who disagree about so many things, went on record around the turn of the millennium predicting that once new media took hold in China a new form of politics would inevitably follow. Others put their faith in a rising middle class, citing

South Korea and Taiwan as examples of authoritarian states that were democratized under pressure from professionals and entrepreneurs.

Any of these things could still happen at some point, but none of the predictions have so far been borne out, just as more recent—and more tentative—forecasts of China experiencing a "color revolution" or counterpart to an Arab Spring-like upheaval have proved inaccurate. One reason for this is that the CCP has worked tirelessly to learn how to avoid precisely such scenarios. Ironically, for this reason, the constant predictions of the CCP's imminent demise may have made its fall *less* rather than *more* likely.

Before Xi Jinping came to power in 2012, many observers thought that while democracy might be a remote possibility for China, some political reforms might at least occur on his watch. Prior to his taking office, outsiders knew very little about Xi, aside from the fact that he came from a princeling family; that, after a stint in the countryside during the Cultural Revolution, he worked his way up the CCP hierarchy largely by playing it safe; and that, in the 1980s, his father had taken stances in favor of greater liberalization. He had a reputation as an economic reformer, and based on this, as well as on his father's one-time criticism of hardliners, some believed that Xi and his second-in-command, Premier Li Keqiang, would pursue moderate political reforms.

Those early hopes have been dashed. Now often compared to both Mao and Deng, Xi has consolidated power by becoming what one writer and historian has called "Chairman of Everything," heading more than a half-dozen "leading small groups" that guide government policy in different areas.[10] He has led an anti-corruption campaign that has toppled many dozens of high-ranking officials and many hundreds of low-ranking ones, turning the CCP upside down. He has also cultivated a personality cult that while more subdued than Mao's is still unlike anything seen since the days of the Great Helmsman: state media sometimes refers to him as *Xi Dada* (literally "Big Daddy Xi," but more commonly translated as "Uncle Xi"), and a series of pop songs and music videos have praised him.[11]

As we have mentioned elsewhere, Xi has also overseen a dramatic crackdown on civil society and tightening of censorship. This "Big Chill" began under Hu Jintao—Xi is not entirely responsible for China's more authoritarian environment—and resembles that taking place in other countries with strongman leaders (e.g., India, Russia, and Turkey).[12] Initially, some commentators suggested that furthering the Big Chill was Xi's method of consolidating his power soon after taking office, with the possibility that the situation would ease in time. That no longer appears likely, and PRC politics have now clearly shifted away not only from democracy but from what now look to be the golden years of the mid-2000s, when controls on legal activism and artistic expression relaxed at least a little bit.

At the Nineteenth Party Congress in the fall of 2017, Xi was appointed to his second five-year term as president, with no clear successor waiting in the wings. Rumors abound that Xi is planning to remain in power after his term ends in 2022. China does have a two-term limit on its presidency, but Xi could abolish that. He could break with the tradition of recent decades and give up the presidency but stay on as party secretary. Or, taking a page from Russian president Vladimir Putin's playbook, he could step down but appoint a docile placeholder for an interim term, then return to office. Even if Xi does leave all his formal positions in 2022, it seems likely that he will continue to exercise power behind the scenes in the manner of Deng or Jiang Zemin, rather than fade away into retirement as Hu Jintao has done.[13]

How powerful is Chinese nationalism?

Media stories about China's "angry youth" (*fenqing*) often give Westerners the impression that the country is filled with fervent nationalists who refuse to accept any criticism of China.

This has led to a notion that Chinese nationalism bolsters the CCP regime. The assumption is that patriotic fervor serves to prop up the official status quo and is a force that the authorities can turn on and off like a tap.

The last two generations of Chinese have indeed been reared on a steady diet of propaganda that emphasizes the humiliations that China suffered at the hands of foreign powers during such events as the Opium War (1839–1842) and the Japanese invasions of the 1930s and 1940s. Young Chinese have been encouraged by the state to be wary of contemporary Western bias against the PRC, as evidenced by such things as unfair presentations of unrest in Xinjiang and Tibet. And sometimes they comply, as in 2016, when they briefly called for a boycott of mangoes from the Philippines after that country won a ruling against China over disputed territory in the South China Sea in an international court (there were also symbolic protests at KFC franchises, as the court was viewed as an arm of the United States).[14] Likewise, they have been encouraged to fill cyberspace with tirades against any Japanese politician who visits the controversial Yasukuni Shrine—a site that honors the souls of Japan's war dead, which includes several Class A war criminals responsible for brutal policies toward the populations of China and other Asian countries.

Nonetheless, it is still overly simplistic to think that the payoff is a mass of angry youths ready to do the PRC's bidding whenever it feels like calling on them. In fact, a recent study found that young Chinese appear to be growing less nationalistic as the years pass, based on the results of a public opinion survey that has been conducted in Beijing at regular intervals since the late 1990s.[15] Even when patriotic education is effective, nationalism remains a double-edged sword, which can buttress the regime but also develop in ways that threaten the political status quo.[16] While it is true that patriotic propaganda has shaped many views of young Chinese, there are complex variations in the way they express their love of country and the degree to which this dovetails with official nationalism. China's leaders are well aware that some of the biggest challenges faced by previous Chinese regimes, including the Tiananmen protests, have been driven in part by patriotic fervor.

They also know that a protest that begins as a loyalist expression of nationalism can devolve into a struggle against their leadership. And they know that oppositional themes can slip in even during demonstrations that are in large part officially stage-managed affairs. This was the case in September 2012, when slogans referring to corruption and a wish for China's current leaders to be more like Mao made appearances in state-sanctioned anti-Japanese protests, one that was associated with a string of tiny uninhabited islands in the East China Sea over which both Beijing and Tokyo claim sovereignty. The authorities know that once mobilized, patriotic fervor always has the potential to work against rather than for them, and this explains why they often douse the flames of youthful nationalist ardor.[17] Thus, Chinese nationalism is a Janus-faced force that moves easily in both loyalist and oppositional directions.

What kind of government will China have in a decade?

Soon after the turn of the millennium, much of the debate about China was framed in terms of the allegedly contrasting visions spelled out in two books: Bruce Gilley's *China's Democratic Future* and Gordon G. Chang's *The Coming Collapse of China*. Both books confidently predicted that China would see dramatic political change, though they disagreed about what that change would be. Now, however, experts more or less agree that China's future path appears to be one of continuity, with the CCP at the helm of an authoritarian state for the indefinite future.

Prior to Xi Jinping's ascension to power, analysts emphasized that continuity did not mean a complete lack of change. They argued for the need to think of the CCP as a protean organization, one which had proved capable of adapting itself to the needs of particular moments. They referred to "adaptive authoritarianism" as the best way to categorize PRC politics.

Some of them noted, moreover, that there were deep roots to this adaptive authoritarianism, which went back much further than the start of the Reform Era.[18] Mao was modifying standard Marxist theory and Leninist visions of the CCP's role as far back as his 1927 "Report on the Hunan Peasant Movement," with its call for Communist organizers to learn from the tactics that villagers were using, rather than seeing themselves as arriving on the scene as teachers of an innately reactionary rural population.

Then, in the 1930s and 1940s, while an opposition organization, the CCP tried many things, including guerrilla warfare strategies, which departed dramatically from traditional practice. And there were departures from orthodoxy again between the late 1950s and mid-1970s, a period that historians now refer to as the era of "High Maoism." For example, many people insisted at that time that a "bad" class status could be passed on from one generation to the next via bloodlines, something that defies the central tenet of Marxism, which links class to one's relationship to the means of production, not to family. The fact is that through its history the CCP, for better or for worse, has shown itself ready to experiment.

Xi Jinping's consolidation of power certainly looks like a step backward toward a more authoritarian time. But even Xi cannot take China back to the days of Mao: despite the frequent comparisons between the two, Xi leads a country far more globally engaged than Mao's China was, and the CCP is far too wary of popular unrest to reverse course too dramatically. Most PRC citizens have grown accustomed to a government that hovers just above their lives but only occasionally descends to intervene in them. The CCP itself must adapt to the limits on its power that the Reform Era brought. So far, it has demonstrated the ability to walk this line, and there is no reason to believe that it will not continue to do so.

What big challenges lie ahead for the CCP?

Five major challenges stand out. These might be called (since the CCP likes slogans with numbers) the Three E's and the Two C's: economy, environment, and energy; and corruption and credibility. We will deal with these issues in the next several questions.

All political leaders have to worry about their country's economy, since people in democracies often vote with their pocketbooks, and in authoritarian settings material issues often decide whether people will take to the streets or stay at home. There is, however, a special dimension to the issue in the PRC today. After three decades of high growth rates that raised the standard of living for hundreds of millions of people and bolstered the CCP's legitimacy, China's economy is slowing and changing.

Although the growth rate remains among the highest in the world (in 2015, China's GDP increased by 6.9 percent, while that of the United States grew at a rate of 2.6 percent), export-oriented manufacturing no longer powers China's economy. Instead, the country is turning to the high-tech and service sectors, as manufacturing jobs move abroad in search of cheaper labor. Donald Trump campaigned on a platform that emphasized the loss of US jobs to China, but China in fact has been suffering the same fate—sometimes even seeing factory jobs move back to the United States.[19] And just as in the US, unemployed factory workers cannot easily shift to the new economy, lacking the education and skills to find new jobs.

This is a problem for the CCP because while the economic boom produced winners and losers, the losers had for decades been able to content themselves with the idea that someday their turn—or their children's turn—would come. Now, that possibility is in jeopardy and its failure to materialize could engender a sense of outrage and desperation among China's low-skilled workers. An end to high growth rates also frustrates the rising expectations of those who had been doing well and assumed that they and their families would continue on an upward trajectory.

The economic slowdown has not yet resulted in widespread, multi-class expressions of discontent, but the CCP is certainly aware that it could. This will be a test for the party, for it follows decades of being both psychologically and practically dependent on high growth rates contributing to a general sense of optimism, and to a belief that, whatever its failings, the CCP has engineered an overall rise in living standards. There are important rumblings of economic discontent, in the form of increasing numbers of strikes, often in sectors that have been hit hard by the slowing growth rates.[20] So far, these have remained circumscribed actions, such as strikes affecting only specific factories or specific occupations, but they are an ongoing source of elite concern. CCP leaders know that their predecessors rose to power in part via struggles fueled by economic factors and that they themselves have been relying heavily on narratives of growth to defend their rule.

What big issues relating to the environment and energy does China face?

Environmental and energy concerns preoccupy all governments, and, as with the economy, they raise a particular set of dilemmas for China's leaders. And the two topics are tightly intertwined—so much so that it makes sense to consider them together.

The good news for China, as it continues to industrialize, is that it has a good supply of two sources of power: coal deposits (thanks to trucks and railroads, the CCP is not disadvantaged the way the Qing were by these being located far from major cities) and water (which can be used to generate electricity via dams). The bad news is that both coal mining and hydraulic projects have devastating side-effects.

The side-effects of coal include high injury and death rates for miners. Although the fatality rate from Chinese mining accidents has fallen dramatically since the early 2000s, when about five thousand miners died on the job every year, the lack of adequate protective gear in many mines employing migrant laborers means that the miners develop black lung disease, a fatal illness when not diagnosed and treated early.[21] Additionally, the use of coal for heating and industry is one of the leading contributors to China's air pollution problems, which cause respiratory diseases across the population and stoke public outrage. The country cannot afford to continue its dependence on coal. PRC leaders know this and are trying to reduce China's consumption, though doing so will be a long-term project.

Hydropower does not produce the air pollution that coal does, and in China's effort to reduce greenhouse-gas emissions it would appear an attractive alternative to coal in energy production. The bad news with hydraulic energy is that massive dams have been unpopular, leading to protests by locals directly affected by the projects, which almost inevitably require villages to be flooded, and worries about the risks of construction errors. Additionally, building dams in the country's southwest—where the best candidate rivers are—involves negotiating with neighboring countries. The region is also prone to earthquakes, and its distance from the energy-thirsty coastal cities makes it difficult to effectively transmit the power produced.[22]

China is expanding its nuclear energy sector. Although there is much public wariness about nuclear power plants after the disaster at Japan's Fukushima plant in 2011, they offer a promising alternative to coal.

The bigger bad news for China on the energy front is that demand for oil is rising rapidly, as the country gains more and more drivers. It needs more and more electricity as well to keep factories humming and provide lights and air conditioning to more and more people living middle-class lifestyles in the country's ever-growing cities. China has oil reserves (some in politically sensitive areas, like Xinjiang, and near Pacific islands that are claimed by both the PRC and either Vietnam or Japan), but not enough to meet its growing needs. In 2015, China surpassed the United States to become the top global importer of crude oil. As with the United States, this demand shapes international behavior: in recent years, China has expanded its influence across Eurasia through its Belt and Road Initiative (BRI). BRI has many dimensions—construction, banking, diplomacy—all aimed at securing China's interests in the region, including its access to natural resources, such as oil from Kazakhstan and gas from Turkmenistan.[23]

Perhaps the biggest resource-related concern, though, is water, and not simply its damming. Due to polluted rivers, melting Himalayan ice caps, and a declining North China water table (which was never in good shape to begin with: per capita water amounts there have long been well below 10 percent of the global average), shortages of drinking water and water for irrigation are already a serious problem and are likely to get much worse in the years to come.

Chinese leaders are not indifferent to the environmental consequences of burning coal or damming rivers. They are also well aware of the damage to the CCP's legitimacy that those consequences pose, both at home and abroad. Air pollution cuts across geographic and class lines: even if wealthier urban residents can afford to purchase expensive air purifiers to run inside their homes, when they go outside they breathe the same toxic air as the poorest citizens. Foreign media routinely run photographs that show the outlines of city buildings dimly visible through dense gray clouds of smog, and in 2013 dubbed an especially bad bout of pollution in Beijing the "Airpocalypse"—hardly the image that China's tourism industry wants to project.

After many years of denying the severity of China's environmental woes (such as insisting that clouds of air pollution were fog rather than smog), the government has recently demonstrated greater willingness to acknowledge and tackle the problem. For example, when in 2008 the US embassy set up its "@BeijingAir" Twitter account, which released real-time air quality data and often showed the pollution as more severe than the Chinese government's numbers, the official Chinese response was one of irritation. Over time, however, popular pressure caused a reversal in government policy. China improved its own air-quality monitoring systems and increased its transparency in this sphere. While bouts of severe pollution persist, the government no longer seems quite so determined to deny their existence.[24]

Environmental concerns are also one area in which there previously existed real potential for US–China cooperation, even as the two sides disagreed on many other issues. The apex of this came in November 2014, when Barack Obama and Xi announced that both countries would commit to a schedule for reducing the emission of greenhouse gases.[25] Under Donald Trump, however, it is unlikely that this cooperation will continue.

Why are corruption and credibility concerns for the CCP?

In his final work report as general secretary, delivered at the Eighteenth Party Congress in November 2012, Hu Jintao warned that corruption could prove to be the CCP's greatest challenge and could undermine the legacy of its achievements.[26] Hu had good reason to issue this warning, since 2012 was a trying year for the CCP where corruption was concerned. In February, the police chief of the massive municipality of Chongqing, in the country's southwest, fled to the US consulate in nearby Chengdu. There he allegedly revealed that Chongqing's party secretary, the charismatic politician Bo Xilai, was involved in an elaborate murder and cover-up. Over the following months, a story of sorts (though many details remain murky) came out. Bo's wife, Gu Kailai, had been involved in illegal business dealings, including money laundering, and may have also carried on an extramarital affair with the English businessman who was her partner in many of those deals, Neil Heywood.

Gu allegedly felt threatened by Heywood and, with one of her household employees, poisoned him and then covered up his murder. While no one claimed that Bo himself was involved in killing Heywood, the murder proved the opportunity that his political opponents needed to take down the formerly rising star (some had previously thought that Bo might have a chance to make it onto the elite Politburo Standing Committee when the Party Congress was held in November). Bo was dismissed from his position as Chongqing party secretary, stripped of party membership, and found guilty of bribery and abuse of power in a 2013 trial. He is now serving a life sentence in prison (as is Gu Kailai).

The shadow of Bo Xilai and his crimes hung heavy over the CCP as Xi Jinping took office. There was also the matter of two exposés by foreign news organizations, the New York Times and Bloomberg News, which documented in impressive detail the ways that the extended families of Xi Jinping and outgoing Premier Wen Jiabao had grown rich through their political connections, and the influence those ties lent them (although neither Xi nor Wen was personally accused of misdeeds).[27] None of this was particularly surprising—the reaction of most Chinese was that the exposés merely confirmed what had already been widely assumed—but the reports were nonetheless damaging to the credibility of the CCP, which has its origins in promises to reduce inequality in society. In retaliation, the government blocked the Bloomberg and New York Times websites and for several years, made it difficult for journalists from those organizations to get visas.

As one of his first acts upon taking office, Xi launched an expansive anti-corruption campaign aimed at clearing party ranks of dirty officials. This is not the first such campaign undertaken by the CCP, but its duration and reach are notable. Party investigators have arrested both "tigers" and "flies" (high-ranking and low-ranking officials, respectively), although the fact that no one with close ties to Xi has been toppled leaves him open to charges that this campaign is an excuse to take down his political rivals. Xi has also imposed a new regime of austerity on CCP officials—for example, by putting an end to lavish banquets floating on a sea of alcohol in favor of a simple "four dishes and a soup" menu at government functions. For these moves, Xi has garnered acclaim from Chinese citizens, who have long been angered by seeing CCP officials use their positions for profit and familial advancement. However, the campaign has also caused paralysis in some government officials, who hesitate to assign contracts or make any moves that might attract the attention of anti-corruption investigators.[28]

High-profile cases of corruption within Chinese politics might not seem to affect the day-to-day lives of ordinary people. What should be of far greater concern to the leadership are the many scandals involving food safety, shoddy construction, and environmental degradation, which are felt at every level of society and stir up anger that cuts across geographic and class boundaries.

Corrupt deals have long been cut between officials and builders, who are either related to one another by blood or linked via *guanxi* (literally, "connections," but in China also implying a strong sense of mutual indebtedness established by friendship, bribery, past favors, having been classmates, or some combination of all of these things). Following the Sichuan earthquake of 2008, anger arose from assertions that school buildings collapsed, killing thousands of children, because of shoddy development and poor safety inspection. These latter issues were believed to be linked to developers with ties to local officials, who cut corners and only perfunctorily adhered to regulations safeguarding the soundness of the structures. It is telling that these claims were immediately believed by a great many people. The fact that some roughly comparable buildings near the schools were left standing added to the plausibility of the criticism, but the main reason that it was accepted initially was just that it is taken for granted that this kind of thing happens all the time. Xi's anti-corruption campaign might stop some of these practices, but it will be difficult to eradicate them at the most local level, where the pull of *guanxi* among family and neighbors could prove a stronger force than fear of the central government's inspection teams.

To date, however, disgust with official corruption has not been strong enough to galvanize nationwide outrage that might result in a repeat of the Tiananmen protests of 1989. And even if Xi's anti-corruption campaign is merely an excuse for purging his political rivals, it still gives the public a sense that the party is doing something to address the problem. The CCP first rose to power in part because people felt its cadres were less corrupt than Nationalist officials; Xi and his allies seem to recognize that they need to bring the party back to its roots.

How can the United States and China adjust to an era in which they are the two superpowers?

The issue of the United States and China sharing the stage as the world's two superpowers is a pressing one. It would be nice to be able to end this book with some simple guidelines for getting beyond, or at least lessening, the kinds of mutual misunderstandings described in chapter 5. While there are no easy solutions, one thing that might help would be a broader appreciation in both countries of the fact that they have much in common.[29]

Some things happening in China today are much like those that happened in the United States when it was industrializing rapidly and rising in global prominence in the late 1800s and early 1900s. Though political figures often present the two countries as completely unlike one another, trends on opposite sides of the Pacific sometimes converge. US and Chinese leaders, for example, often present their countries as founded in struggles against empires and opposed to all forms of imperialism—yet both the United States and the PRC have been accused of taking actions that seem imperialistic. There are also intellectuals based in Europe and India, who note that, despite all the efforts Washington and Beijing make to present themselves as dissimilar, both seem to share a penchant for going to great lengths to protect access to oil—a point that some American critics of US foreign policy sometimes note as well—and that US and Chinese delegates on the UN Security Council are among the most likely to block that body's efforts to censure their allies.

What other kinds of things do China and the United States have in common?

There are many other parallels, some of which concern precisely the things that Americans are fond of criticizing about the PRC. One journalist has noted in an article about the "instant cities" of China, where many factories use machines that are pirated versions of US machines, that the United States' industrial takeoff was fueled in part by just this sort of reverse engineering that allowed businessmen in early US boomtowns to make use, for free, of patented British technologies.[30] And as one US historian has pointed out, in the late 1800s it was the United States that was often seen by Europeans, as China is now often seen by Americans, as a place that produced inferior and sometimes downright dangerous goods and issued pirated editions of best-sellers (Charles Dickens complained bitterly about how many unauthorized versions of his books were sold across the Atlantic).[31]

Something else the countries have in common is that between the late 1800s and mid-1900s, the United States built railways and highway systems on a grand scale, which connected parts of the country that were previously cut off from one another and were sometimes hailed as engineering marvels, just as China has been doing with its construction of the world's longest high-speed rail network. As a 2008 *Scientific American* article put it: the China of the twenty-first century "is a developing country undergoing an energy transformation unprecedented in human history, but fired by an engineering

optimism reminiscent of the US in the 1950s."[32] Others have referred to the early twenty-first century as China's Gilded Age,
a time when economic growth and urbanization are driving
the country forward, as they did the United States at the dawn
of the twentieth century.[33]

That was also the era when the United States hosted its
first World's Fairs and first Olympics. And as one anthropol-
ogist of sports reminds us, when the United States first got to
hold the games in 1904 (previously, the event had only been
held in Europe), some foreign commentators assumed, as they
did again during the lead-up to 2008, that the International
Olympic Committee had made a terrible mistake in letting the
Olympics be hosted by a country that might have a booming
economy but was clearly not ready for prime time.[34]

Is this an argument for Americans to refrain from all criticism of China?

An increased awareness of similarities such as those just
noted need not prevent or even discourage Americans from
criticizing things that occur in China, and vice versa. But it
does suggest that it would be useful to be mindful of parallels
between things happening in China now and things that
happened in this country in the past, and that, as a result,
when Americans take the PRC to task for certain things, a "bit
of empathy might even be in order," as one US historian put
it in an essay on comparisons between the two nations.[35] If the
residents of each superpower thought as much about what
they have in common as what makes them different, it could
even help increase the odds that, whichever way the criticisms
fly across the Pacific, they will be delivered in a less arrogant
and patronizing fashion than has sometimes been the case in
the past.

Another thing that could help ease US–China misunderstandings would simply be for people in each country to
know more about the people living in the other. We hope that

US readers who have made it to the end of this book feel that they now know a few more basic things about the people of the PRC than they did when they read its first pages. And we look forward to the day when we can point Chinese friends toward a comparable work that tries to tell them, in a similar spirit of seeking to normalize the experiences of a large and exotic-seeming anti-imperialist empire that stands by the Pacific, "everything they need to know" about the United States.

NOTES

Chapter 1

1. There are several different systems for romanizing Chinese. We use what has become most common of these: the *pinyin* system adopted by the PRC in 1979. When there is a widely known alternative in the older Wade-Giles system, it follows in parentheses so that readers will be familiar with it if they encounter the term in other texts.

2. For further information on Confucius and other early thinkers discussed in this section, see Benjamin I. Schwartz, *The World of Thought in Ancient China* (Cambridge, MA: Harvard University Press, 1985); the bibliography of this synthetic work will lead the interested reader to good translations of the relevant primary texts. For translated excerpts of key philosophers, see Wm. Theodore de Bary, Irene Bloom et al., eds., *Sources of Chinese Tradition, Volume I*, 2nd ed. (New York: Columbia University Press, 2000).

3. On the origin of fortune cookies, see Jennifer 8. Lee, "Solving a Riddle Wrapped in a Mystery Inside a Cookie," *New York Times*, January 16, 2008, http://www.nytimes.com/2008/01/16/dining/16fort.html (accessed August 5, 2017).

4. Lionel M. Jensen, *Manufacturing Confucianism* (Durham, NC: Duke University Press, 1997).

5. On misconceptions about the Great Wall, see Arthur Waldron, *The Great Wall of China: From History to Myth* (Cambridge: Cambridge University Press, 1992).

6. K. E. Brashier, ed., *The First Emperor: Selections from the Grand Historian* (Oxford: Oxford University Press, 2009).

7. For background on the New Culture movement and relevant citations, see Chow Tse-tsung, *The May Fourth Movement: Intellectual Revolution in Modern China* (Cambridge, MA: Harvard University Press, 1960), and Rana Mitter, *A Bitter Revolution: China's Struggle with the Modern World* (Oxford: Oxford University Press, 2004).

8. This language shows up in many places; see, for example, "Xi Elaborates Chinese Civilization at College of Europe," Xinhua News Agency, April 2, 2014, http://english.qstheory.cn/news/201404/t20140402_336425.htm (accessed August 5, 2017).

9. "President Xi Stresses National Unity, Religious Harmony in Ningxia," Xinhua News Agency, July 20, 2016, http://english.cri.cn/12394/2016/07/20/2561s934991.htm (accessed August 5, 2017).

10. Lionel M. Jensen, "Culture Industry, Power, and the Spectacle of China's 'Confucius Institutes,'" in *China in and Beyond the Headlines*, Timothy B. Weston and Lionel M. Jensen, eds. (Lanham, MD: Rowman & Littlefield, 2012), 271–299, quote 283.

11. Elizabeth Redden, "Chicago to Close Confucius Institute," *Inside Higher Ed*, September 26, 2014, https://www.insidehighered.com/news/2014/09/26/chicago-severs-ties-chinese-government-funded-confucius-institute (accessed August 5, 2017); "Another Confucius Institute to Close," *Inside Higher Ed* (October 1, 2014), https://www.insidehighered.com/quicktakes/2014/10/01/another-confucius-institute-close (accessed August 5, 2017).

12. James Carter and Jeffrey Wasserstrom, "To Understand China's President Xi Jinping, Don't Look to Mao Tse-tung, Look to Chiang Kai-shek," *Los Angeles Times*, May 24, 2016, http://www.latimes.com/opinion/op-ed/la-oe-carter-wasserstrom-china-xi-chiang-20160524-snap-story.html (accessed August 5, 2017).

13. Yu Dan, *Confucius from the Heart: Ancient Wisdom for the Modern World* (London: MacMillan, 2009); Sheila Melvin, "Yu Dan and China's Return to Confucius," *New York Times*, August 29, 2007, http://www.nytimes.com/2007/08/29/arts/29iht-melvin.1.7298367.html (accessed August 5, 2017); Evan Osnos, "Confucius Comes Home," *The New Yorker*, January 13, 2014, http://www.newyorker.com/magazine/2014/01/13/

confucius-comes-home (accessed August 5, 2017). See also Sam
Crane, "A Talk with Yu Dan," *The Useless Tree*, July 31, 2014,
http://uselesstree.typepad.com/useless_tree/2014/07/a-talk-
with-yu-dan-1.html (accessed August 5, 2017) and his previous
writings about Yu Dan linked to in that post.

14. Andrew Jacobs, "Confucius Statue Vanishes Near Tiananmen
Square," *New York Times*, April 22, 2011, http://www.nytimes.
com/2011/04/23/world/asia/23confucius.html (accessed
August 5, 2017).

15. Chris Buckley, "Leader Taps into Chinese Classics in Seeking to
Cement Power," *New York Times*, October 11, 2014, http://www.
nytimes.com/2014/10/12/world/leader-taps-into-chinese-classics
-in-seeking-to-cement-power.html (accessed August 5, 2017).

16. This term is used as the title of the most influential book on
the topic, Kenneth L. Pomeranz, *The Great Divergence: China,
Europe, and the Making of the Modern World Economy* (Princeton,
NJ: Princeton University Press, 2000).

17. Peter Zarrow, "China: Vicissitudes of Definitions," *Perspectives
on History*, September 2016, https://www.historians.org/
publications-and-directories/perspectives-on-history/september-
2016/china-vicissitudes-of-definitions (accessed August 5, 2017).

Chapter 2

1. Li Xueqin, *Eastern Zhou and Qin Civilizations* (New Haven,
CT: Yale University Press, 1985), 12–15.

2. John King Fairbank and Merle Goldman, *China: A New History*
(Cambridge, MA: Belknap Press of Harvard University Press,
1998), 59.

3. Patricia Buckley Ebrey, *The Inner Quarters: Marriage and the Lives
of Chinese Women in the Sung Period* (Berkeley: University of
California Press, 1993).

4. Dorothy Ko, *Teachers of the Inner Chambers: Women and Culture
in Seventeenth-Century China* (Stanford: Stanford University
Press, 1995); Susan Mann, *The Talented Women of the Zhang Family*
(Berkeley: University of California Press, 2007).

5. James Millward, *The Silk Road: A Very Short Introduction*
(New York: Oxford University Press, 2013); Mark Edward Lewis,
China's Cosmopolitan Empire: The Tang Dynasty (Cambridge, MA:
Harvard University Press, 2009).

6. In *1421: The Year China Discovered America* (New York: William Morrow, 2003), Gavin Menzies claims that Zheng He circumnavigated the globe and reached the Americas decades before Christopher Columbus did. Nearly all scholars dispute the version of Zheng He's voyages provided by Menzies; for an account of Zheng He's voyages that conforms to the conventional wisdom, see Louise Levathes, *When China Ruled the Seas: The Treasure Fleet of the Dragon Throne, 1405–1433* (New York: Simon and Schuster, 1994).

7. Peter Ward Fay, *The Opium War, 1840–1842* (Chapel Hill: University of North Carolina Press, 1975); and James Polachek, *The Inner Opium War* (Cambridge, MA: Council on East Asian Studies, Harvard University, 1992).

8. Susan Naquin, *Millenarian Rebellion in China: The Eight Trigrams Uprising of 1813* (New Haven, CT: Yale University Press, 1976).

9. Daniel Overmyer, *Folk Buddhist Religion: Dissenting Sects in Late Imperial China* (Cambridge, MA: Harvard University Press, 1976).

10. Fairbank and Goldman, *China: A New History*, 189–191.

11. Stephen R. Platt, *Autumn in the Heavenly Kingdom: China, the West, and the Epic Story of the Taiping Civil War* (New York: Knopf, 2012) is a major study of the insurrection, which emphasizes ties as well as parallels between the Chinese and American civil wars.

12. Henrietta Harrison, *The Making of the Republican Citizen: Political Ceremonies and Symbols in China, 1911–1929* (Oxford: Oxford University Press, 2000).

13. Harrison Salisbury, *The New Emperors: China in the Era of Mao and Deng* (New York: Avon Books, 1992); similar imagery is employed in George Paloczi-Horvath, *Mao Tse-tung: Emperor of the Blue Ants* (London: Secker & Warburg, 1962).

14. John Garnaut, *The Rise and Fall of the House of Bo: How a Murder Exposed the Cracks in China's Leadership* (Beijing: Penguin China, 2012).

15. "China's Future: Xi Jinping and the Chinese Dream," *The Economist*, May 4, 2013, http://www.economist.com/news/leaders/21577070-vision-chinas-new-president-should-serve-his-people-not-nationalist-state-xi-jinping (accessed August 9, 2017), cover titled "Party Like It's 1799." On "red" families being spared from the anti-corruption drive, see Geremie Barmé, "Tyger! Tyger! A Fearful Symmetry," *China Story*, October 16, 2014, https://www.thechinastory.org/2014/10/tyger-tyger-a-fearful-symmetry/ (accessed August 9, 2017).

16. Kerry Brown, *CEO, China: The Rise of Xi Jinping* (London: I.B. Tauris, 2016). It is worth noting that Brown himself employed imperial imagery in an earlier book, which dealt with both Bo Xilai and Xi Jinping, *The Red Emperors: Power and the Princelings in China* (London: I.B. Taurus, 2014).

Chapter 3

1. Marie-Claire Bergère, *Sun Yat-sen*, trans. Janet Lloyd (Stanford: Stanford University Press, 1998).
2. James E. Sheridan, *China in Disintegration: The Republican Period in Chinese History, 1912–1949* (New York: Free Press, 1975).
3. Rana Mitter, *A Bitter Revolution: China's Struggle with the Modern World* (Oxford: Oxford University Press, 2004).
4. Lu Xun, *The Real Story of Ah-Q and Other Tales of China: The Complete Fiction of Lu Xun*, trans. Julia Lovell (New York: Penguin, 2010).
5. For a fictionalized reference to Lu Xun's elevated status in Mao's China, see "Lu Xun," a story in Yu Hua's collection *China in Ten Words* (New York: Pantheon Books, 2011).
6. Arif Dirlik, *The Origins of Chinese Communism* (Oxford: Oxford University Press, 1989).
7. Richard Rigby, *The May Thirtieth Movement: Events and Themes* (Canberra: Australia National University Press, 1980).
8. Donald Jordan, *The Northern Expedition: China's National Revolution of 1926–1928* (Honolulu: University of Hawaii Press, 1976); and, for the Workers' Uprisings, see Elizabeth J. Perry, *Shanghai on Strike: The Politics of Chinese Labor* (Stanford: Stanford University Press, 1993).
9. Despite his prominence in the revolutionary movement, today Wang Jingwei is primarily remembered in China as a traitor for his decision to collaborate with the Japanese during World War II as the head of a puppet government based in Nanjing. See Rana Mitter, *Forgotten Ally: China's World War II, 1937–1945* (New York: Houghton Mifflin Harcourt, 2013) for a thorough assessment of Wang's life and political career.
10. Edgar Snow, *Red Star Over China* (1938; repr., New York: Grove Press, 1968).
11. John King Fairbank and Merle Goldman, *China: A New History* (Cambridge, MA: Belknap Press of Harvard University Press,

1998), 305; R. Keith Schoppa, *Revolution and Its Past: Identities and Change in Modern Chinese History* (Upper Saddle River, NJ: Prentice Hall, 2002), 235.

12. Benjamin Yang, *From Revolution to Politics: Chinese Communists on the Long March* (Boulder, CO: Westview, 1990).

13. Schoppa, *Revolution and Its Past*, 257.

14. Suzanne Pepper, *Civil War in China: The Political Struggle, 1945–1949* (Berkeley: University of California Press, 1978).

15. Premier Zhou Enlai (Chou En-lai) quotation from John Gardner, "The *Wu-fan* Campaign in Shanghai," in *Chinese Communist Politics in Action*, ed. A. Doak Barnett (Seattle: University of Washington Press, 1969), 477.

16. Jonathan D. Spence, *The Search for Modern China*, 2nd ed. (New York: Norton, 1999), 498–513.

17. Susan Glosser, *Chinese Visions of Family and State, 1915–1953* (Berkeley: University of California Press, 2003).

18. Gail Hershatter, *The Gender of Memory: Rural Women and China's Collective Past* (Berkeley: University of California Press, 2011), chapter 7.

19. For a wide selection of propaganda posters depicting Mao in many different ways, see Stefan Landsberger's Chinese Posters website http://chineseposters.net/ (accessed August 12, 2017).

20. Mark Selden, ed., *The People's Republic of China: A Documentary History of Revolutionary Change* (New York: Monthly Review Press, 1979), 213.

21. Spence, *The Search for Modern China*, 553; and Carl Riskin, "Seven Questions about the Chinese Famine of 1959–61," *China Economic Review* 9, no. 2 (1998): 111–124.

22. Alexander C. Cook, *The Cultural Revolution on Trial: Mao and the Gang of Four* (New York: Cambridge University Press, 2016).

23. For more on the "dragon lady" trope in Chinese history, see Paul French, "Tale of the Dragon Lady," *Foreign Policy*, June 26, 2012, http://www.foreignpolicy.com/articles/2012/06/26/tale_of_the_dragon_lady (accessed August 12, 2017). Bo Xilai's wife, Gu Kailai, has frequently been cast in a similar light since he was purged from power and she was arrested for murder in 2012.

24. Jung Chang and Jon Halliday, *Mao: The Unknown Story* (New York: Knopf, 2005).

25. For scholarly responses to Chang and Halliday, see Gregor Benton and Lin Chun, eds., *Was Mao Really a Monster? The*

Academic Response to Chang and Halliday's Mao: The Unknown Story (London and New York: Routledge, 2010). Sinologist Frank Dikötter has also equated Mao with Hitler in his influential books on China in the 1950s and '60s; for a brief commentary, see Tom Phillips, "Great Helmsman or Ruinous Dictator? China Remembers Mao, 40 Years after Death," *The Guardian*, September 8, 2016, https://www.theguardian.com/world/2016/sep/08/great-helmsman-dictator-china-anniversary-mao-40-years-after-death (accessed August 12, 2017).

26. Cary Huang, "Mao Portraits in Anti-Japan Protests a Cause for Concern for Leaders," *South China Morning Post*, September 20, 2012, http://www.scmp.com/news/china/article/1040993/mao-portraits-anti-japan-protests-cause-concern-leaders (accessed August 12, 2017).

27. Mao plays a starring role in the many Cultural Revolution-themed restaurants that have appeared in Chinese cities over the past decade-plus. These eateries make capitalist-style profits by drawing on curiosity about and nostalgia for China's communist past. See Adam Century, "Chongqing Restaurants Serve Cultural Revolution Nostalgia," *The Atlantic*, November 4, 2013, https://www.theatlantic.com/china/archive/2013/11/chongqing-restaurants-serve-cultural-revolution-nostalgia/281100/, (accessed August 15, 2017); Jennifer Hubbert, "Revolution Is a Dinner Party: Cultural Revolution Restaurants in Contemporary China," *China Review* 5, no. 2 (Fall 2005): 125–150.

Chapter 4

1. For extensive galleries of PRC propaganda posters, see http://chineseposters.net/ (accessed October 14, 2017).

2. "Jiang of Jiang Hall," *The Economist*, July 30, 2016, http://www.economist.com/news/china/21702777-it-began-mockery-former-leader-now-it-has-strange-life-its-own-jiang-jiang-hall (accessed October 14, 2017).

3. Carl Minzner, "China After the Reform Era," *Journal of Democracy* 26, no. 3 (June 2015), 129–143.

4. Mei Fong, *One Child: The Story of China's Most Radical Experiment* (New York: Houghton Mifflin Harcourt, 2016).

5. For a lively discussion of the "period police," see Lijia Zhang's excellent memoir *"Socialism Is Great!": A Worker's Memoir of the New China* (New York: Atlas, 2008).

6. Chris Buckley, "China Ends One-Child Policy, Allowing Families Two Children," *New York Times*, October 29, 2015, https://www.nytimes.com/2015/10/30/world/asia/china-end-one-child-policy.html (accessed October 14, 2017).

7. Mara Hvistendahl, *Unnatural Selection: Choosing Boys Over Girls, and the Consequences of a World Full of Men* (New York: PublicAffairs, 2011).

8. On the "one-child policy," see Tyrene White, *China's Longest Campaign* (Ithaca, NY: Cornell University Press, 2006); Susan Greenhalgh, *Just One Child: Science and Policy in Deng's China* (Berkeley: University of California Press, 2008); and Jeffrey Wasserstrom, "Resistance to the One-Child Family," *Modern China* 10, no. 3 (July 1984), 345–374.

9. Ezra F. Vogel, *Deng Xiaoping and the Transformation of China* (Harvard, MA: Belknap Press of Harvard University Press, 2011).

10. See Jonathan Unger, ed., *The Pro-Democracy Protests in China: Reports from the Provinces* (Armonk, NY: M.E. Sharpe, 1991).

11. George Black and Robin Munro, *Black Hands of Beijing: Lives of Defiance in China's Democracy Movement* (New York: John Wiley, 1993).

12. Louisa Lim, *The People's Republic of Amnesia: Tiananmen Revisited* (New York: Oxford University Press, 2014).

13. On the rediscovery of "The Communist Manifesto" as a text that has prescient things to say about globalization, and citations to comments on this score by people such as Thomas Friedman, who is not, by any means, associated with the far left, see "Afterword: Is the *Manifesto* Still Relevant?" in Philip Gaster, ed., *The Communist Manifesto: A Road Map to History's Most Important Political Document* (Chicago: Haymarket, 2005).

14. See, for example, Edward Friedman and Barrett L. McCormick, eds., *What If China Doesn't Democratize?* (Armonk, NY: M. E. Sharpe, 2000), and Bruce Dickson, *China's Red Capitalists: The Party, Entrepreneurs, and Prospects for Political Change* (Cambridge: Cambridge University Press, 2003).

15. Julia Lovell, *The Opium War: Drugs, Dreams and the Making of China* (London: Picador, 2011) contains an extended discussion of the post-1989 patriotic education movement.

16. Mao Zedong, "A Single Spark Can Start a Prairie Fire," January 5, 1930, https://www.marxists.org/reference/archive/mao/selected-works/volume-1/mswv1_6.htm (accessed December 22, 2017).

17. Peter Lorentzen, "Designing Contentious Politics in Post-1989 China," *Modern China*, 43, no. 5 (September 2017), 459–493.

18. For a typical case in point, see "China Dismisses Local Leaders after Angry Protest," July 25, 2009, http://www.sandiegouniontribune.com/sdut-china-unrest-072509-2009jul25-story.html (accessed October 14, 2017).

19. Tania Branigan, "China's Jasmine Revolution: Police but No Protesters Line Streets of Beijing," *The Guardian*, February 27, 2011, https://www.theguardian.com/world/2011/feb/27/china-jasmine-revolution-beijing-police (accessed September 15, 2017).

20. Austin Ramzy, "Protests Return to Wukan, Chinese Village that Once Expelled Its Officials," *New York Times*, June 20, 2016, https://www.nytimes.com/2016/06/21/world/asia/china-wukan-protest.html (accessed October 14, 2017); Stephen McDonell, "China's Protest Village of Wukan Crushed," BBC News, September 13, 2016, http://www.bbc.com/news/blogs-china-blog-37351737 (accessed October 14, 2017).

21. Kevin J. O'Brien, "Rural Protest," *Journal of Democracy* 20, no. 3 (July 2009), 25–28.

22. Ian Johnson, "Focusing on Religious Oppression in China Misses the Big Picture," CNN, February 28, 2017, http://www.cnn.com/2017/02/28/opinions/china-religion-johnson (accessed October 14, 2017).

23. Clifford Coonan, "China and Vatican Edge Closer to Deal to Improve Relations," *Irish Times*, October 31, 2016, http://www.irishtimes.com/news/world/asia-pacific/china-and-vatican-edge-closer-to-deal-to-improve-relations-1.2849718 (accessed October 14, 2017); Sinica Podcast, "Ian Johnson on the Vatican and China," December 29, 2016, http://supchina.com/podcasts/ian-johnson-vatican-china/ (accessed October 14, 2017).

24. Ian Johnson, "Practicing Falun Gong Was a Right, Ms. Chen Said, Up to Her Last Day," *Wall Street Journal*, April 20, 2000, http://www.wsj.com/articles/SB956186343489597132 (accessed October 14, 2017).

25. Jessica Gelt, "Falun Gong, Banned in China, Finds a Loud Protest Voice in the U.S. Through Shen Yun Dance Troupe," *Los Angeles*

Times, April 9, 2016, http://www.latimes.com/entertainment/arts/la-et-cm-shen-yun-20160409-story.html (accessed October 14, 2017).

26. David Ownby, "China's War against Itself," *New York Times*, February 15, 2001, http://www.nytimes.com/2001/02/15/opinion/china-s-war-against-itself.html (accessed October 14, 2017). Ownby ends with the claim that Falun Gong's "evocation of a different vision of Chinese tradition and its contemporary value is now so threatening to the state and party because it denies them the sole right to define the meaning of Chinese nationalism, and perhaps of Chineseness." See also Ownby's book *Falun Gong and the Future of China* (New York: Oxford University Press, 2008).

27. Louisa Lim and Jeffrey Wasserstrom, "The Gray Zone: How Chinese Writers Elude Censors," *New York Times*, June 15, 2012, http://www.nytimes.com/2012/06/17/books/review/how-chinese-writers-elude-censors.html (accessed October 14, 2017).

28. For a pair of thoughtful but often diametrically opposed assessments of Mo's writing and qualifications for winning the Nobel Prize, each by a respected specialist in Chinese literature, see Jeffrey Wasserstrom's interview with Sabina Knight, "China's Latest Laureate: Chinese Lit Scholar Answers Questions about Mo Yan," *Los Angeles Review of Books*, October 12, 2012, https://lareviewofbooks.org/article/chinas-latest-laureate-chinese-lit-scholar-answers-questions-about-mo-yan/ (accessed October 14, 2017); and Perry Link, "Does This Writer Deserve the Prize?" *New York Review of Books*, December 6, 2012, http://www.nybooks.com/articles/archives/2012/dec/06/mo-yan-nobel-prize/ (accessed October 14, 2017).

29. Perry Link, "Liu Xiaobo's Empty Chair," *New York Review of Books* blog, December 13, 2010, http://www.nybooks.com/blogs/nyrblog/2010/dec/13/nobel-peace-prize-ceremony-liu-xiaobo/ (accessed October 14, 2017).

30. Tom Phillips, "Activists Call on China to Release Liu Xiaobo for Cancer Treatment Abroad," *The Guardian*, July 9, 2017, https://www.theguardian.com/world/2017/jul/09/liu-xiaobo-tells-foreign-doctors-he-wants-to-leave-china-for-treatment (accessed September 16, 2017); Chris Buckley, "Liu Xiaobo's Fate Reflects Fading Pressure on China Over Human Rights," *New York Times*,

July 13, 2017, https://www.nytimes.com/2017/07/13/world/
asia/liu-xiaobo-china-human-rights.html (accessed September
16, 2017); Perry Link, "The Passion of Liu Xiaobo," *New York
Review of Books*, July 13, 2017, http://www.nybooks.com/daily/
2017/07/13/the-passion-of-liu-xiaobo/ (accessed September
16, 2017).

31. Chen's story is recounted in Evan Osnos, *Age of Ambition: Chasing
Fortune, Truth, and Faith in the New China* (New York: Farrar,
Straus and Giroux, 2014).

32. Leta Hong Fincher, "China's Feminist Five," *Dissent*, Fall 2016,
https://www.dissentmagazine.org/article/china-feminist-five
(accessed October 14, 2017).

33. Maura Elizabeth Cunningham and Jeffrey N. Wasserstrom,
"Authoritarianism: There's an App for That," *Chinese Journal of
Communication* 5, no. 1 (March 2012), 43–48.

34. "Big Vs and Bottom Lines," *The Economist*, August 31, 2013,
http://www.economist.com/news/china/21584385-authorities-
move-against-some-chinas-most-vocal-microbloggers-big-vs-
and-bottom-lines (accessed October 14, 2017).

35. The first English-language discussion of the "The Great Firewall"
metaphor we know of appeared in an important early analysis
of the Chinese Internet by Geremie R. Barmé and Sang Ye,
"The Great Firewall of China," *Wired* 5, no. 6 (June 1997), 138–
150, available at https://www.wired.com/1997/06/china-3/
(accessed October 14, 2017).

36. See, for example, Andrew Leonard, "Tiananmen's Bloody
Lessons for Tehran," posted at the Salon.com blog "How the
World Works," June 19, 2009, http://www.salon.com/2009/06/
19/tiananmen_and_tehran/ (accessed October 14, 2017); and
Tony Karon, "Iran: Four Ways the Crisis May Resolve," *Time*,
June 18, 2009, http://content.time.com/time/world/article/
0,8599,1905356,00.html (accessed October 14, 2017). Thanks
to Xiao Qiang for clarifying some of the similarities between
Chinese and Iranian efforts to control the Internet—and stressing
the point of the lesser sophistication and comparative slowness
of the moves typically made by the authorities in Tehran as
compared to their counterparts in Beijing.

37. For a recent example of a non-authoritarian country that
has taken steps to block websites that are seen to promote
pornography or terrorism, see Suzanne (Edward Shelley,

translator), "France Sees Sharp Rise in Blocked and De-Listed Websites," Global Voices Advox, March 6, 2017, https://advox. globalvoices.org/2017/03/06/france-sees-sharp-rise-in-blocked- and-de-listed-websites/ (accessed October 14, 2017)

38. Many relevant discussions of Chinese Internet censorship (with occasional posts about similar practices in other countries) can be found at the following Web sites: RConversation (http:// rconversation.blogs.com), China Digital Times (http:// chinadigitaltimes.net/), and the Hong Kong-based China Media Project (http://cmp.hku.hk/) (all accessed October 14, 2017).

39. Craig S. Smith, "The *New York Times* vs. The 'Great Firewall' of China," *New York Times*, March 31, 2017, https://www.nytimes. com/2017/03/31/insider/the-new-york-times-vs-the-great- firewall-of-china.html (accessed September 16, 2017); Tania Branigan, "China Relaxes Internet Censorship for Olympics," *The Guardian*, August 1, 2008, https://www.theguardian.com/ world/2008/aug/01/china.olympics (accessed September 16, 2017).

40. On just how tightly connected the worlds of industry and government can become in contemporary China, consider this summary that Kenneth Pomeranz provides of the blurring of lines between state and private actors in the Three Gorges Dam project: "While this organization [into parent and subsidiary companies that are given control over different parts of the world's biggest hydraulic project] allows dam-builders to take advantage of private capital markets and corporate organization, their links to the state remain crucial. Huaneng Power Group, which holds development rights for the Lancang (Upper Mekong), was until recently headed by Li Xiaopeng, son of former Premier (and chief advocate of the Three Gorges project) Li Peng. (The younger Li, who like so many other Chinese leaders has a background in engineering, has since moved on to become deputy governor of Shanxi, with responsibility for industry and coal mining.) His sister, Li Xiaolin, is the CEO of Huaneng's most important subsidiary, China Power International Development Ltd. (a Hong Kong corporation)." Kenneth Pomeranz, "The Great Himalayan Watershed," *New Left Review* 58 (July/August 2009), 5–39.

41. Minxin Pei, "The Dark Side of China's Rise," *Foreign Policy*, March/April 2006, http://foreignpolicy.com/2009/10/20/

the-dark-side-of-chinas-rise/ (accessed October 14, 2017), makes
the case for using the concept of crony capitalism to think about
China, but also describes it as a neo-Leninist state.

42. William J. Dobson, *The Dictator's Learning Curve: Inside the Global
Battle for Democracy* (New York: Anchor Books, 2012).

43. For an early use of "Market-Leninism," see Nicholas Kristof,
"China Sees 'Market-Leninism' as Way to Future," *New York
Times,* September 6, 1993, http://www.nytimes.com/1993/
09/06/world/china-sees-market-leninism-as-way-to-future.
html (accessed October 14, 2017). Several people have used and
given particular spins to the term "Capitalism with Chinese
Characteristics" over the years. It has been featured, for
example, in the name of an essay by Shawn Breslin, "Capitalism
with Chinese Characteristics: The Public, the Private and the
International," Murdoch University Asia Research Centre,
Working Paper 104 (August 2004); then in the title of a conference
that Scott Kennedy convened at Indiana University, "Capitalism
with Chinese Characteristics: China's Political Economy in
Comparative and Theoretical Perspectives" (May 19–20,
2006); and after that in the title of Yasheng Huang's *Capitalism
with Chinese Characteristics: Entrepreneurship and the State*
(Cambridge: Cambridge University Press, 2008).

44. Pallavi Aiyar, "Urumqi Is Not Too Different from Godhra,"
Business Standard, July 16, 2009, http://www.business-standard.
com/article/opinion/pallavi-aiyar-urumqi-is-not-too-different-
from-godhra-109071600030_1.html (accessed November 5, 2017).

45. Geeta Anand, "India's Air Pollution Rivals China's as World's
Deadliest," *New York Times,* February 14, 2017, https://www.
nytimes.com/2017/02/14/world/asia/indias-air-pollution-
rivals-china-as-worlds-deadliest.html (accessed November
5, 2017).

Chapter 5

1. Important works on this subject include Harold Isaacs, *Scratches
on Our Minds: American Views of China and India* (Armonk, NY:
M. E. Sharpe, 1997), the reissue of a seminal work first published
in 1958; Jonathan D. Spence, *The Chan's Great Continent: China
in Western Minds* (New York: W. W. Norton, 1999); Colin
Mackerras, *Sinophiles and Sinophobes: Western Views on China*

(New York: Oxford University Press, 2001), which includes
an excellent selection of primary sources; and, most recently,
John Pomfret, *The Beautiful Country and the Middle Kingdom*
(New York: Henry Holt, 2016).

2. Ethan Gutman, "A Tale of the New China: What I Saw at the
   American Embassy in Beijing," *Weekly Standard*, May 24, 1999, 23;
   the author writes of feeling "heady and faint just for being there
   [in Beijing]: the capital of the next century's Superpower, the
   center of the world for a day, its youth, Borg-like in their unified
   loathing of our flag and our little plot." (This last word refers to
   the fact that there was a widespread assumption in China then,
   as there still is, that the bombing of the Belgrade embassy had
   been intentional, not a mistake.) The same author invokes the
   sci-fi notion of the "Chinese Borg" again in "Who Lost China's
   Internet?" *Weekly Standard*, February 25, 2002, 24.

3. See, for example, Jeffrey N. Wasserstrom, "Student Protests in
   Fin-de-Siècle China," *New Left Review* 237 (September/October
   1999): 52–76.

4. A fascinating discussion of the variation within the category
   of Han can be found in Sara L. Friedman, "Embodying
   Civility: Civilizing Processes and Symbolic Citizenship in
   Southeastern China," *Journal of Asian Studies* 63, no. 3 (August
   2004): 687–718.

5. On the wide variety of foot-binding practices, see Dorothy
   Ko, *Cinderella's Sisters: A Revisionist History of Footbinding*
   (Berkeley: University of California Press, 2007).

6. For the names containing radicals linked to animals that Han
   Chinese have used to refer to ethnic groups imagined to be
   less civilized, see Dru Gladney, *Dislocating China: Reflections on
   Muslims, Minorities, and Other Subaltern Subjects* (London: C.
   Hurst, 2004), 35. For a similar process, involving prejudice
   against Han migrants to the city who are seen as inferior and
   referred to by some locals as "Subei swine," for example, see
   Emily Honig, *Creating Chinese Ethnicity: Subei People in Shanghai,
   1850–1980* (New Haven, CT: Yale University Press, 1992).

7. Geremie R. Barmé and Jeremy Goldkorn, eds., "*Suzhi*," *The China
   Story Yearbook 2013: Civilising China* (Canberra: Australian Centre
   on China in the World, 2013), xiii.

8. Carl Haub, "China Releases First 2010 Census Results,"
   Population Reference Bureau, May 2011, http://www.prb.org/

Articles/2011/china-census-results.aspx (accessed September 28, 2017).

9. For sample efforts to bring *Brave New World*'s relevance into discussions of the PRC, as either a supplement to or substitute for the still more prevalent treatments of China as an Orwellian Big Brother state, see Jeffrey Wasserstrom, "China's Brave New World," *Current History* 102, 665 (September 2003): 266–269; Howard W. French, "Letter from China: What If Beijing Is Right?" *New York Times*, November 2, 2007, http://www.nytimes.com/2007/11/02/world/asia/02iht-letter.1.8162318.html (accessed September 28, 2017); Rana Mitter, *Modern China: A Very Short Introduction* (Oxford: Oxford University Press, 2007); and Jeremy Goldkorn, "Dystopia and Censorship," Danwei, August 27, 2009, http://www.danwei.org/internet_culture/dystopia_and_censorship.php (accessed September 28, 2017).

10. For more on this letter, see Jeffrey Wasserstrom, *China's Brave New World—And Other Tales for Global Times* (Bloomington: Indiana University Press), 125.

11. See, for example, John J. Thacik, "China's Orwellian Internet," *Heritage Foundation* Backgrounder #1806 (October 8, 2004), http://www.heritage.org/asia/report/chinas-orwellian-internet (accessed September 28, 2017); and William Pesek, "Web Porn Won't Hurt China as Much as Orwell Will," Bloomberg News, June 22, 2009, http://www.smh.com.au/business/web-porn-wont-hurt-china-as-much-as-orwell-will-20090621-csvc.html (accessed September 28, 2017).

12. Jeremy Goldkorn, "Dystopia and Censorship." This piece is framed around an excerpt from an important August 26, 2009, op-ed of Goldkorn's that appeared in the *Daily Telegraph*, "China's Internet, the Wild, Wild East," but it ran, as he notes, without a final line that alluded to Orwell and Huxley, an omission he rectified in the version that he posted at the URL provided here.

13. China Digital Times (CDT) monitors and publishes confidential press instructions, which include both directives to avoid certain events or topics and instructions that media must cover certain other events or topics. See a full list of such instructions leaked to CDT since 2011 at the site's "Directives from the Ministry of Truth" http://chinadigitaltimes.net/china/

directives-from-the-ministry-of-truth/ (accessed September 28, 2017). For a recent analysis of state newspapers running identical front pages, see David Bandurski, "Pointing to the Future, Parroting the Past: Front Pages of Chinese State Media after the 19th Party Congress," *Hong Kong Free Press*, October 27, 2017, https://www.hongkongfp.com/2017/10/28/pointing-future-parroting-past-front-pages-chinese-state-media-19th-party-congress/ (accessed November 5, 2017).

Chapter 6

1. Charles Hutzler, "China to Slim Down Its Military," *Wall Street Journal*, September 3, 2015, http://www.wsj.com/articles/china-to-slim-down-military-1441252819 (accessed October 4, 2017).

2. Joyce Lau, "Thousands Protest China's Plans for Hong Kong Schools," *New York Times*, July 29, 2012, http://www.nytimes.com/2012/07/30/world/asia/thousands-protest-chinas-curriculum-plans-for-hong-kong-schools.html (accessed October 4, 2017); "Hong Kong Backs Down Over Chinese Patriotism Classes," BBC, September 8, 2012, http://www.bbc.com/news/world-asia-china-19529867 (accessed October 4, 2017).

3. Cary Huang, "Does Taiwan Still Matter to Mainland China?" *South China Morning Post*, January 16, 2016, http://www.scmp.com/comment/insight-opinion/article/1901786/does-taiwan-still-matter-mainland-china (accessed October 4, 2016).

4. Sara L. Friedman, *Exceptional States: Chinese Immigrants and Taiwanese Sovereignty* (Berkeley: University of California Press, 2015), 7.

5. "One Year On: Impact of 'Sunflower' Movement Protests in Taiwan Continues to Blossom," *South China Morning Post*, March 17, 2015, http://www.scmp.com/news/china/article/1740013/one-year-impact-sunflower-movement-protests-taiwan-continue-blossom (accessed October 4, 2017).

6. "Migrant Workers and Their Children," *China Labour Bulletin*, http://www.clb.org.hk/content/migrant-workers-and-their-children (accessed October 4, 2017).

7. Leslie T. Chang, *Factory Girls: From Village to City in a Changing China* (New York: Spiegel & Grau, 2008), 12.

8. Maura Elizabeth Cunningham, "The Vulnerability of China's Left-Behind Children," *Wall Street Journal* China Real Time

Report, March 21, 2014, http://blogs.wsj.com/chinarealtime/
2014/03/21/the-vulnerability-of-chinas-left-behind-children/
(accessed October 4, 2017).

9. Tom Miller, *China's Urban Billion: The Story Behind the Biggest Migration in Human History* (London: Zed Books, 2012); "The Great Sprawl of China," *The Economist*, January 24, 2015, http://www.economist.com/news/china/21640396-how-fix-chinese-cities-great-sprawl-china (accessed October 4, 2017).

10. Geremie R. Barmé has referred to Xi as "Chairman of Everything" numerous times. See, for example, Geremie R. Barmé, "Introduction: Under One Heaven," *China Story Yearbook 2014: Shared Destiny*, eds. Geremie R. Barmé, Linda Jaivin, and Jeremy Goldkorn (Canberra: Australian National University Centre on China in the World, 2014), xx.

11. "Xi Jinping's Leadership: Chairman of Everything," *The Economist*, April 2, 2016, http://www.economist.com/news/china/21695923-his-exercise-power-home-xi-jinping-often-ruthless-there-are-limits-his (accessed October 4, 2017); "Visualizing China's Anti-Corruption Campaign," ChinaFile, January 21, 2016, http://www.chinafile.com/infographics/visualizing-chinas-anti-corruption-campaign (accessed October 4, 2017); Tom Phillips, "Singing Xi's Praises: Chorus of Chinese Pop Songs Celebrate President," *The Guardian*, March 30, 2016, https://www.theguardian.com/world/2016/mar/30/xi-jinping-chorus-of-chinese-pop-songs-celebrate-president (accessed October 4, 2017).

12. Evan Osnos, "China: The Big Chill," *The New Yorker*, April 1, 2011, https://www.newyorker.com/news/evan-osnos/china-the-big-chill (accessed October 3, 2017).

13. Chris Buckley, "Xi Jinping May Delay Picking China's Next Leader, Stoking Speculation," *New York Times*, October 4, 2016, https://www.nytimes.com/2016/10/05/world/asia/china-president-xi-jinping-successor.html (accessed October 4, 2017).

14. Richard Curt Kraus and Jeffrey Wasserstrom, "Mangoes, K-Pop and KFC: Chinese Nationalism Today," *The TLS*, September 29, 2016, http://www.the-tls.co.uk/articles/public/mangoes-k-pop-kfc/ (accessed October 4, 2017).

15. Alastair Iain Johnson, "Is Chinese Nationalism Rising? Evidence from Beijing," *International Security* 41, no. 3 (Winter 2016/17): 7–43.

16. For a smart, accessibly written scholarly account, see Stanley
    Rosen, "Contemporary Chinese Youth and the State," *Journal
    of Asian Studies* 68, no. 2 (May 2009): 359–369; while for state-
    of-the-art journalism on the same subject, see Evan Osnos,
    "Angry Youth," *The New Yorker*, July 28, 2008, http://www.
    newyorker.com/reporting/2008/07/28/080728fa_fact_osnos
    (accessed October 4, 2017). Anti-Japanese protests in August
    and September 2012 once again led to a slew of commentaries
    on the complexities of Chinese nationalism; one of the most
    intriguing is Helen Gao, "Diaoyu in Our Heart: The Revealing
    Contradictions of Chinese Nationalism," *The Atlantic*, August 22,
    2012, http://www.theatlantic.com/international/archive/2012/
    08/diaoyu-in-our-heart-the-revealing-contradictions-of-chinese-
    nationalism/261422/ (accessed October 4, 2017). On state efforts
    to combat nationalism that does not fall in line with official
    sentiments, see Lucy Hornby, "China Battles to Control Growing
    Online Nationalism," *Financial Times*, January 8, 2017, https://
    www.ft.com/content/5ae7b358-ce3c-11e6-864f-20dcb35cede2
    (accessed October 4, 2017).

17. See Suisheng Zhao, "China's Pragmatic Nationalism: Is
    It Manageable?" *Washington Quarterly* 29, no. 1 (Winter
    2005–2006): 131–144.

18. On this issue, see Elizabeth J. Perry and Sebastian Heilmann,
    eds., *Mao's Invisible Hand: The Political Foundations of Adaptive
    Governance in China* (Cambridge, MA: Harvard University
    Press, 2011).

19. GDP growth rates from the World Bank, http://data.worldbank.
    org/indicator/NY.GDP.MKTP.KD.ZG (accessed October 4, 2017).
    Michael Schuman, "Is China Stealing Jobs? It Might Be Losing
    Them, Instead," *New York Times*, July 22, 2016, https://www.
    nytimes.com/2016/07/23/business/international/china-jobs-
    donald-trump.html (accessed October 4, 2017).

20. "Strikes and Protests by Chinese Workers Soar to Record Heights
    in 2015," *China Labour Bulletin*, July 1, 2016, http://www.clb.
    org.hk/en/content/strikes-and-protests-china%E2%80%99s-
    workers-soar-record-heights-2015 (accessed October 4, 2017).

21. "Mining Safety: Shaft of Light," *The Economist*, July 18, 2015,
    http://www.economist.com/news/china/21657824-coal-
    fuels-chinas-boom-becoming-less-deadly-extract-shaft-light
    (accessed October 4, 2017); Sim Chi Yin, "A Miner's China
    Dream," ChinaFile, June 10, 2015, http://www.chinafile.com/

video/miners-china-dream (accessed October 4, 2017); Fu Danni, "Casualties of China's Coal Addiction," Sixth Tone, December 22, 2016, http://www.sixthtone.com/news/1727/casualties-of-chinas-coal-addiction (accessed October 4, 2017).

22. Kenneth Pomeranz, "The Great Himalayan Watershed," *New Left Review* 58 (July/August 2009): 5–39; Beth Walker and Liu Qin, "China's Shift from Coal to Hydro Comes at a Heavy Price," *chinadialogue*, July 27, 2015, https://www.chinadialogue.net/article/show/single/en/8093-China-s-shift-from-coal-to-hydro-comes-at-a-heavy-price (accessed October 4, 2017); Tom Phillips, "Joy as China Shelves Plans to Dam 'Angry River,'" *The Guardian*, December 2, 2016, https://www.theguardian.com/world/2016/dec/02/joy-as-china-shelves-plans-to-dam-angry-river (accessed October 4, 2017).

23. Keith Johnson, "China Tops U.S. as Biggest Oil Importer," *Foreign Policy*, May 11, 2015, http://foreignpolicy.com/2015/05/11/china-tops-u-s-as-biggest-oil-importer-middle-east-opec-sloc/ (accessed October 4, 2017); William T. Wilson, "China's Huge 'One Belt, One Road' Initiative Is Sweeping Central Asia," *The National Interest*, July 27, 2017, http://nationalinterest.org/feature/chinas-huge-one-belt-one-road-initiative-sweeping-central-17150 (accessed October 4, 2017).

24. David Roberts, "How the US Embassy Tweeted to Clear Beijing's Air," *Wired*, March 6, 2015, https://www.wired.com/2015/03/opinion-us-embassy-beijing-tweeted-clear-air/ (accessed October 4, 2017).

25. David Biello, "Everything You Need to Know about the U.S.–China Climate Change Agreement," *Scientific American*, November 12, 2014, https://www.scientificamerican.com/article/everything-you-need-to-know-about-the-u-s-china-climate-change-agreement/ (accessed October 4, 2017).

26. Ananth Krishnan, "Corruption, Reforms Dominate China's Communist Party Meet Opener," *The Hindu*, November 8, 2012, http://www.thehindu.com/news/international/corruption-reforms-dominate-chinas-communist-party-meet-opener/article4076505.ece (accessed October 4, 2017).

27. "Xi Jinping Millionaire Relations Reveal Fortunes of Elite," Bloomberg News, June 29, 2012, http://www.bloomberg.com/news/2012-06-29/xi-jinping-millionaire-relations-reveal-fortunes-of-elite.html (accessed October 4, 2017); David Barboza, "Billions in Hidden Riches for Family of Chinese Leader," *New York Times*, October 25, 2012, http://www.nytimes.com/

2012/10/26/business/global/family-of-wen-jiabao-holds-a-hidden-fortune-in-china.html (accessed October 4, 2017).

28. Andrew Hall Wedeman, "Xi Jinping's Tiger Hunt," China Policy Institute: Analysis, March 17, 2014, https://cpianalysis.org/2014/03/17/xi-jinpings-tiger-hunt/ (accessed October 4, 2017); Chris Buckley, "Q. and A.: Andrew Wedeman on the Fight Against Corruption in China," *New York Times*, November 6, 2014, https://sinosphere.blogs.nytimes.com/2014/11/06/q-and-a-andrew-wedeman-on-the-fight-against-corruption-in-china/ (accessed October 4, 2017); Yanzhong Huang, "The Anti-Corruption Drive and Risk of Policy Paralysis in China," Asia Unbound, April 24, 2015, http://blogs.cfr.org/asia/2015/04/24/the-anti-corruption-drive-and-risk-of-policy-paralysis-in-china/ (accessed October 4, 2017); Andrew Wedeman, "Four Years On: Where Is Xi Jinping's Anti-Corruption Drive Headed?" China Policy Institute: Analysis, September 19, 2016, https://cpianalysis.org/2016/09/19/four-years-on-where-is-xi-jinpings-anti-corruption-drive-headed/ (accessed October 4, 2017).

29. See Bruce Cummings, *Dominion from Sea to Sea: Pacific Ascendancy and American Power* (New Haven, CT: Yale University Press, 2009), which is primarily about the United States, as its title suggests, but ends with comments about the desirability of embracing the heretical notion that the United States and China have much in common.

30. Peter Hessler, "China's Instant Cities," June 2007, *National Geographic*, http://ngm.nationalgeographic.com/2007/06/instant-cities/hessler-text (accessed October 4, 2017).

31. Stephen Mihm, "A Nation of Outlaws," in Kate Merkel-Hess et al., *China in 2008: A Year of Great Significance* (Lanham, MD: Rowman & Littlefield, 2009).

32. David Biello, "Can Coal and Clean Air Co-exist in China?" *Scientific American*, August 4, 2008, http://www.scientificamerican.com/article.cfm?id=can-coal-and-clean-air-coexist-china (accessed October 4, 2017).

33. Evan Osnos, *Age of Ambition: Chasing Fortune, Truth, and Faith in the New China* (New York: Farrar, Straus and Giroux, 2014), 6.

34. Susan Brownell, "America's and Japan's Olympic Debuts: Lessons for Beijing 2008 (and the Tibet Controversy)," *The Asia Pacific Journal: Japan Focus*, #2754, 2008, http://apjjf.org/-Susan-Brownell/2754/article.html (accessed October 4, 2017).

35. Mihm, "A Nation of Outlaws," 278.

FURTHER RESOURCES

Part I: General

Broad college surveys of Chinese history used to be dubbed "Yao to Mao" courses, playing upon the names of one of the legendary sage kings of the prerecorded past and the first paramount leader of the PRC. Useful, accessibly written general overviews that take you from Yao to Mao include Patricia Ebrey, *The Cambridge Illustrated History of China* (Cambridge University Press, 1999) and John K. Fairbank and Merle Goldman, *China: A New History* (Harvard University Press, 1998). Other useful works with a large but not quite as large temporal sweep include Charles Hucker, *China to 1850: A Short History* (Stanford University Press, 1978), a model of conciseness; Jonathan Spence, *The Search for Modern China,* 3rd ed. (W. W. Norton, 2013), a model of fluent and erudite narrative prose that begins with the rise to power of the Qing Dynasty (1644–1912); Jeffrey Wasserstrom, ed., *The Oxford Illustrated History of Modern China* (Oxford University Press, 2016), which contains chapters by leading scholars of the late imperial and revolutionary periods; and Howard W. French, *Everything Under the Heavens: How the Past Helps Shape China's Push for Global Power* (Knopf, 2017), which surveys the last several centuries of Chinese history with a focus on the country's relationships with its Pacific neighbors. Some of these books appeared a quarter-century ago or more, and hence, while still valuable, do not take on board the very latest findings of academic specialists. Below, however, readers will find many specialized works that were published in the twenty-first century and are informed by the very latest scholarship.

Chapter 1

One of the best general introductions to the ideas of Confucius, Mencius, and competing philosophers of their eras remains Benjamin Schwartz, *The World of Thought in Ancient China* (Harvard University Press, 1985). For a collection of translations of selected works by these thinkers, all carefully introduced, see Wm. Theodore de Bary and Irene Bloom, eds., *Sources of Chinese Tradition, Volume 1: From Earliest Times to 1600* (Columbia University Press, 1999). Arthur Waley's *Three Ways of Thought in Ancient China* (Stanford University Press, 1939) remains a good work to turn to for getting a basic appreciation of the similarities and differences between the worldviews of Mencius and the Daoists and Legalists (referred to by Waley as "Realists"), who lived at the same time as he did or a century or so before or after him; it is filled with translations of particularly engaging passages (and sometimes, especially in the case of the Daoist Zhuang Zi, ones that are amusing as well as illuminating). For background on the First Emperor and his posthumous reputations, see K. E. Brashier's excellent introduction to Sima Qian, *The First Emperor: Selections from the Historical Records*, trans. Raymond Dawson (Oxford University Press, 2007). On the complex process by which the ideas of Confucius and his followers evolved into something known as "Confucianism," see Lionel M. Jensen, *Manufacturing Confucianism: Chinese Traditions and Universal Civilization* (Duke University Press, 1997). For background on the veneration of Confucius in the past and the return of temples and statues honoring him in recent years, see Julia K. Murray, " 'Idols' in the Temple: Icons and the Cult of Confucius," *Journal of Asian Studies*, 68.2 (May 2009), 371–411. For a more positive assessment of the meaning of the revival of interest in Confucius and his thought than we provide, see Daniel A. Bell, *China's New Confucianism* (Princeton University Press, 2008); for a valuable, appreciative yet critical look at this book, see Timothy Cheek, "The Karaoke Classics: A View from Inside China's Confucian Revival," *Literary Review of Canada* (November 2008), http://reviewcanada.ca/reviews/2008/11/01/the-karaoke-classics/. For a variety of short takes on the opening ceremonies of the Beijing Games, including in some cases analysis of the allusions to Confucius made during it, see the relevant essays by Geremie R. Barmé, Lee Haiyan, and others in Kate Merkel-Hess, Kenneth L. Pomeranz, and Jeffrey N. Wasserstrom, eds., *China in 2008: A Year of Great Significance* (Rowman and Littlefield, 2009; hereafter *China in 2008*). For a critical evaluation of Xi Jinping's use of the classics, see Sam Crane, "Philosopher King," *Los Angeles Review of Books*

China Channel (November 17, 2017), https://chinachannel.org/2017/
11/17/philosopher-king/; Crane's blog "Useless Tree" (http://www.
uselesstree.typepad.com/) is a valuable resource for readers seeking
wide-ranging discussions of Chinese philosophy. For varied takes on
Chinese democratic traditions (and the related theme of Chinese human
rights traditions), see Andrew J. Nathan, *Chinese Democracy* (University
of California Press, 1986), Marina Svensson, *Debating Human Rights in
China* (Rowman and Littlefield, 2002), and Joseph W. Esherick and Jeffrey
N. Wasserstrom, "Acting Out Democracy: Political Theater in Modern
China," *Journal of Asian Studies*, 49.4 (November 1990), 835–865.

Chapter 2

Readers looking for scholarly but accessible surveys of specific dynasties,
which are informed by up-to-date studies, can turn to the Harvard
University Press series *History of Imperial China* edited by Timothy Brook.
The six volumes in this important undertaking include three by Mark
Lewis, *The Early Chinese Empires: Qin and Han* (2007), *China's Cosmopolitan
Empire: The Tang Dynasty* (2009), and *China Between Empires: The Northern
and Southern Dynasties* (2011); Dieter Kuhn, *The Age of Confucian Rule: The
Song Transformation of China* (2009); Timothy Brook, *The Troubled
Empire: China in the Yuan and Ming Dynasties* (2010); and William T. Rowe,
China's Last Empire: The Great Qing (2009). On imperial China's multiple
and reciprocal connections across Eurasia, see Peter Frankopan, *The
Silk Roads: A New History of the World* (Knopf, 2016). For an overview
of late imperial China, see Frederic E. Wakeman Jr., *The Fall of Imperial
China* (Free Press, 1975). Engaging recent accounts of mid-nineteenth-
century events include Julia Lovell, *The Opium War: Drugs, Dreams,
and the Making of China* (Picador, 2011); Robert Bickers, *The Scramble for
China: Foreign Devils in the Qing Empire, 1832–1914* (Penguin, 2011); and
Stephen R. Platt, *Autumn in the Heavenly Kingdom: China, The West, and
the Epic Story of the Taiping Civil War* (Knopf, 2012). These three books are
introduced, compared, and contrasted in Maura Elizabeth Cunningham,
"Forgetting and Remembering: New Books on China and the West in
the Nineteenth Century," *World History Connected*, October 2012, http://
worldhistoryconnected.press.illinois.edu/9.3/br_cunningham.html.
On the Boxers, see Joseph W. Esherick, *The Origins of the Boxer Uprising*
(University of California Press, 1988); Paul A. Cohen, *History in Three
Keys: The Boxers as History, Myth, and Experience* (Columbia University
Press, 1997); and Robert Bickers and R. G. Tiedemann, eds., *The Boxers,*

China, and the World (Rowman and Littlefield, 2007). For an accessible, fictionalized version of the events of 1900, see *Boxers and Saints*, a two-volume graphic novel by Gene Luen Yang (First Second, 2013). For similarities and differences between Chinese imperial rulers and the leaders of the Communist Party, along with many other subjects of interest, see Geremie R. Barmé, *The Forbidden City* (Profile Books, 2008).

Chapter 3

There are many valuable books that cover some or all of the events and people discussed in this section, and which provide information that is more detailed than could be provided here, yet are still very accessibly written. Most also contain footnotes, bibliographical essays, or both, that will point the reader to still more specialized studies. See, for example, Rana Mitter, *A Bitter Revolution: China's Struggle with the Modern World* (Oxford University Press, 2005), which is particularly strong on the legacy of the May 4th Movement; Jonathan Fenby, *The Penguin History of Modern China: The Fall and Rise of a Great Power, 1850–2009* (Penguin, 2008), which is especially useful for its handling of political events involving the Nationalist and Communist Parties and the personalities of their leaders; John Gittings, *The Changing Face of China* (Oxford University Press, 2006), which is very effective in tracing events of the Mao years (1949–1976); Peter Zarrow, *China in War and Revolution, 1895–1949* (Routledge, 2005), which analyzes intellectual trends in a sophisticated manner; and Pamela Crossley, *The Wobbling Pivot, China since 1800: An Interpretive History* (Wiley, 2010), which has a distinctive focus on the relationship between central authorities and local communities.

For the lives and times of the two main Nationalist leaders, see Marie-Claire Bergère, *Sun Yat-sen* (Stanford University Press, 2000) and Jay Taylor, *The Generalissimo: Chiang Kai-shek and the Struggle for Modern China* (Harvard University Press, 2009). Rana Mitter also devotes considerable attention to Chiang in *Forgotten Ally: China's World War II, 1937–1945* (Houghton Mifflin Harcourt, 2013).

The literature on Mao is enormous. A good comprehensive biography is Alexander V. Pantsov and Steven I. Levine, *Mao: The Real Story* (Simon & Schuster, 2012). Two valuable short books are Timothy Cheek's *Mao Zedong and the Chinese Revolutions: A Brief History with Documents* (Bedford, 2002), which includes translations of some of the leader's most significant tracts; and Rebecca Karl's *Mao Zedong and China in the Twentieth-Century World* (Duke, 2010). Important essays on various aspects of Mao's life and legacy, written by leading specialists in diverse specific fields, can be found in Timothy Cheek, ed., *A Critical Introduction to Mao* (Cambridge University Press, 2010). For Lu Xun, see *The Real Story of Ah-Q and Other Tales of China: The Complete Fiction of Lu Xun* (Penguin, 2009), which comes with an excellent overview of his life and writings by translator Julia Lovell, and, for recent approaches to the author, Jon Eugene von Kowallis's review essay, "Lu Xun on Our Minds: The Post-Socialist Reappraisal," *Journal of Asian Studies*, 73.3 (August 2014), 581–587. For bottom-up looks at the Mao period, see Edward Friedman et al., *Chinese Village, Socialist State* (Yale University Press, 1993); Jeremy Brown and Matthew D. Johnson, eds., *Maoism at the Grassroots: Everyday Life in China's Era of High Socialism* (Harvard University Press, 2015); and, for the experiences of women in the early PRC, Gail Hershatter, *The Gender of Memory: Rural Women and China's Collective Past* (University of California Press, 2011). For a sense of what it was like to grow up in the era, see the reminisces in various sections of Yu Hua, *China in Ten Words*, trans. Allan Barr (Pantheon, 2011), and Xueping Zhong et al., *Some of Us: Chinese Women Growing up in the Mao Era* (Rutgers, 2011); and on the Marriage Law, see Susan Glosser, *Chinese Visions of Family and State, 1915–1953* (University of California Press, 2003).

On the lead-up to and playing out of the Cultural Revolution, see Roderick MacFarquhar and Michael Schoenhals, *Mao's Last Revolution* (Harvard University Press, 2006); the powerful documentary film Carma Hinton and Geremie R. Barmé, dirs., *Morning Sun* (2005) www.morningsun.org; and Richard C. Kraus, *The Cultural Revolution: A Very Short Introduction* (Oxford, 2012), which is a marvel of erudite concision. Three notable books published as the fiftieth anniversary of the start and fortieth anniversary of the end of the Cultural Revolution were being marked are Frank Dikötter, *The Cultural Revolution: A People's History, 1962–1976* (Bloomsbury, 2016), which is especially interesting on developments in the countryside during the final years of Mao's life; Chris Berry, Patricia Thornton, and Peidong Sun, *The Cultural Revolution: Memories and Legacies 50 Years On* (Cambridge University Press, 2016), which initially appeared as a special issue of *China Quarterly* and showcases work by many prominent scholars; and Guobin Yang, *The Red Guard Generation and Political Activism in China* (Columbia University Press, 2016). On student actions in China's capital, see Andrew G. Walder, *Fractured Rebellion: The Beijing Red Guard Movement* (Harvard University Press, 2009); for the cultural, artistic, and gendered dimensions of the period, see Harriet Evans and Stephanie Donald, eds., *Picturing Power in* the People's Republic of China: Posters of the Cultural Revolution (Rowman and Littlefield, 1999), a richly illustrated collection of essays, as well as Barbara Mittler, A Continuous Revolution: Making Sense of Cultural Revolution Culture (Harvard University Asia Center, 2012); for violent events in the countryside, see Yang Su, Collective Killings in Rural China during the Cultural Revolution (Cambridge University Press, 2011); and for a fascinating look at the international impact of the most important text associated with the event, see Alexander Cook, ed., The Little Red Book: A Global History (Cambridge University Press, 2014. On the Great Leap Famine, see Yang Jisheng, Tombstone: The Great Chinese Famine, 1958–1962, trans. Stacy Mosher and Guo Jian (FSG, 2012); Zhou Xun, ed., The Great Famine in China, 1958–1962: A Documentary History (Yale, 2012); and Frank Dikötter, Mao's Great Famine (Bloomsbury, 2010). For Mao's reputation since 1976 and debates about the meaning of his life and deeds, see Geremie R. Barmé, Shades of Mao: The Posthumous Cult of the Great Leader (M. E. Sharpe, 1996) and Lin Chun and Gregor Benton, eds., Was Mao Really a Monster? (Routledge, 2009).

Part II: General

Some of the best books to turn to get a sense of how China has been changing in recent years and of the human side of the country's dramatic transformations are the works of freelance writers and journalists, such as Ian Johnson, Michelle Dammon Loyalka, Zha Jianying, Duncan Hewitt, Leslie T. Chang, Michael Meyer, Peter Hessler, Sang Ye, Evan Osnos, Rob Schmitz, Helen Gao, and Alec Ash. Three good books to begin with are Hessler's Country Driving: A Journey through China from Farm to Factory (HarperCollins, 2010); a collection of Sang Ye's Studs Terkel–like interviews with ordinary Chinese from many walks of life, translated superbly by Geremie R. Barmé as China Candid: The People of the People's Republic of China (University of California Press, 2006); and Zha's Tide Players: The Movers and Shakers of a Rising China (New Press, 2011). See also Angilee Shah and Jeffrey Wasserstrom, eds., Chinese Characters: Profiles of Fast-Changing Lives in a Fast-Changing Land (University of California Press, 2012), which offers a sampling of short pieces by a diverse array of gifted writers, including several mentioned above. A still-valuable introduction to both Chinese politics and US–China relations is provided by Susan Shirk, China: Fragile Superpower (Oxford University Press, 2007), while an engaging presentation of basic facts about the country can be found in Stephanie Donald and Robert

Benewick, *The State of China Atlas*, rev. ed. (University of California Press, 2009), and a useful survey of recent political and economic trends and dilemmas is Jonathan Fenby, *Tiger Head, Snake Tails: China Today, How It Got There and Where It is Heading* (Simon and Schuster, 2013). For an informative collection of writings by leading experts on Chinese politics, society, eds., the economy, and more, see Jennifer Rudolph and Michael Szonyi, *The China Questions: Critical Insights into a Rising Power* (Harvard University Press, 2018).

Chapter 4

For general introductions to the post-1976 period, see Richard Baum, *Burying Mao: Chinese Politics in the Era of Deng Xiaoping*, rev. ed. (Princeton University Press, 1996), which is particularly good on high politics; Timothy Cheek, *Living with Reform: China Since 1989* (Zed, 2007), which is good on cultural and intellectual developments; Ezra Vogel, *Deng Xiaoping and the Transformation of China* (Harvard, 2011), which approaches the period through the prism of the life of its most powerful figure; and Julian Gewirtz, *Unlikely Partners: Chinese Reformers, Western Economists, and the Making of Global China* (Harvard University Press, 2017), which covers the history of economic reforms after Mao's death. On Democracy Wall and related events, see Andrew J. Nathan, *Chinese Democracy* (University of California Press, 1986), Merle Goldman, *Sowing the Seeds of Democracy in China: Political Reform in the Deng Xiaoping Decade* (Harvard University Press, 1994), and Geremie R. Barmé and John Minford, eds., *Seeds of Fire: Chinese Voices of Conscience* (Hill & Wang, 1988). On the events and intellectual trends that led up to Tiananmen, see the final chapter of Jeffrey N. Wasserstrom, *Student Protests in Twentieth-Century China: The View from Shanghai* (Stanford University Press, 1991), various chapters in Elizabeth J. Perry and Jeffrey N. Wasserstrom, eds., *Popular Protest and Political Culture in Modern China*, 2nd ed. (Westview, 1994), and Perry Link, *Evening Chats in Beijing* (W. W. Norton, 1993).

The literature on Tiananmen itself is enormous, even if limiting one's purview to English-language materials; there are also voluminous publications in Chinese and important studies and document collections in French and other Western languages. A good selection of relevant works is available at www.tsquare.tv, a Web site created to accompany the excellent documentary *The Gate of Heavenly Peace* (1996), directed by Carma Hinton and Richard Gordon. See also Craig Calhoun, *Neither Gods nor Emperors: Students and the Struggle for Democracy in*

China (University of California Press, 1997), and Philip J. Cunningham, *Tiananmen Moon: Inside the Chinese Student Uprising of 1989* (Rowman and Littlefield, 2009); for the massacre itself and some key figures in the struggle, George Black and Robin Munro, *Black Hands of Beijing* (Wiley, 1993); for the actions of the army, Timothy Brook, *Quelling the People* (Stanford University Press, 1998); for the writings of participants, Han Minzhu, ed., *Cries for Democracy* (Princeton University Press, 1990), and Geremie R. Barmé and Linda Jaivin, eds., *New Ghosts, Old Dreams* (Crown, 1992); for events outside of Beijing, Jonathan Unger, ed., *The Chinese Democracy Movement: Reports from the Provinces* (M. E. Sharpe, 1991); and for perspective on the unrest of high-ranking Communist Party officials, Zhao Ziyang, *Prisoner of the State: The Secret Journal of Zhao Ziyang* (Simon and Schuster, 2009), as well as Liang Zhang, comp., *The Tiananmen Papers* (Public Affairs, 2001). For the legacy of 1989 in popular memory, see Louisa Lim, *The People's Republic of Amnesia: Tiananmen Revisited* (Oxford University Press, 2014); on the post-1989 lives of protesters, see Rowena Xiaoqing He, *Tiananmen Exiles: Voices of the Struggle for Democracy in China* (Palgrave Macmillan, 2014).

For the ability of the CCP to remain in power since 1989 and social changes in the intervening years, see Peter Hays Gries and Stanley Rosen, eds., *State and Society in 21st-Century China* (Routledge, 2004), especially the chapter on legitimacy by Vivienne Shue; Elizabeth J. Perry and Mark Selden, eds., *Chinese Society: Change, Conflict and Resistance*, 2nd ed. (Routledge, 2003), which is particularly good on protests since Tiananmen; David Shambaugh, *China's Communist Party: Atrophy and Adaptation* (University of California Press, 2008), which excels in illuminating efforts the CCP made to learn from the fall of other state socialist regimes; Sebastian Heilmann and Elizabeth J. Perry, eds., *Mao's Invisible Hand: The Political Foundations of Adaptive Governance in China* (Harvard, 2011), which reminds us of how ready to experiment the CCP has been throughout its history; Richard McGregor, *The Party: The Secret World of China's Communist Rulers* (Harper, 2010), which is strong on the ways that political, business, and military concerns intertwine; the contributions by Andrew J. Nathan (probably the leading proponent of the "resilient authoritarianism" idea) and others in a special section on China since 1989 included in the July 2009 issue of *The Journal of Democracy*; and Carl Minzner, "China After the Reform Era," *The Journal of Democracy*, June 2015, 129–143 and *End of An Era: How China's Authoritarian Revival is Undermining Its Rise* (Oxford University Press, 2018). On Falun Gong, see David Ownby, *Falun Gong and the Future of China* (Oxford University Press, 2008).

On religion in the PRC, see Yoshiko Ashiwa and David L. Wank, eds., *Making Religion, Making the State: The Politics of Religion in Modern China* (Stanford University Press, 2009); various articles, reviews, and commentaries by Ian Johnson, as well as his book, *The Souls of China: The Return of Religion After Mao* (Pantheon, 2017); and the materials by Evan Osnos and others that are gathered together on the Web site for the Frontline documentary "Jesus in China," www.pbs.org/frontlineworld/stories/china_705/.

On the complex landscape of intellectual life in contemporary China and the need to think in terms of more than just a simple divide between dissidents and apologists for the regime, see the compendium of views showcased in important collections edited by Wang Chaohua, *One China, Many Paths* (Verso, 2005), and by Gloria Davies, *Voicing Concerns* (Rowman and Littlefield, 2001). See also Michael Dutton, *Streetlife China* (Cambridge University Press, 1999); Geremie R. Barmé, *In the Red* (Columbia University Press, 1999), which remains the best overall account of the strategies that artists and intellectuals use to navigate in the gray zone between officially allowed and overtly repressed forms of cultural activities (for an updated account of this issue, see Louisa Lim and Jeffrey Wasserstrom, "The Gray Zone: How Chinese Writers Elude Censors," *New York Times*, June 5, 2012); many posts on *New Yorker* correspondent Evan Osnos's blog "Letter from China," including "Jia Zhangke and Rebiya Kadeer," www.newyorker.com/online/blogs/evanosnos/2009/07/jia-zhangke-rebiya-kadeer.html; and Sebastian Veg, "China's Embryonic Public Sphere," *Current History* (September 2015), 203–209.

On Mo Yan see Perry Link, "Does this Writer Deserve the Prize?" *New York Review of Books*, December 6, 2012; and, for a contrasting view, Charles Laughlin, "What Mo Yan's Detractors Get Wrong," *ChinaFile*, December 11, 2012, http://www.chinafile.com/what-mo-yans-detractors-get-wrong. On Liu Xiaobo, see the collection of his writings edited by Perry Link, Tienchi Martin-Liao, and Liu Xia, working with various translators, *No Enemies, No Hatred: Selected Essays and Poems* (Harvard, 2012), which comes with an extended introduction by Link, as well as Ian Johnson, "Liu Xiaobo: The Man Who Stayed," *NYR Daily*, July 14, 2017, http://www.nybooks.com/daily/2017/07/14/liu-xiaobo-the-man-who-stayed/, an essay written at the time of Liu's death that puts his life and work into a broader historical context.

On Chinese birth control campaigns, see Susan Greenhalgh, *Just One Child: Science and Policy in Deng's China* (University of California Press, 2008); Mei Fong, *One Child: The Story of China's Most Radical*

Experiment (Houghton Mifflin Harcourt, 2016); Mara Hvistendahl, *Unnatural Selection: Choosing Boys Over Girls, and the Consequences of a World Full of Men* (Public Affairs, 2011); and, for a summary, Harriet Evans, "The Little Emperor Grows Selfish," *New Statesman*, January 1, 2005, http://www.newstatesman.com/node/161178. On the meaning of the Olympics, see Susan Brownell, *Beijing's Games: What the Olympics Mean to China* (Rowman and Littlefield, 2008).

On comparing China and India, see the insightful writings of Pankaj Mishra (e.g., "It's a Round World After All: India, China, and the Global Economy," *Harper's*, August 2007, 83–88) and Pranab Bardhan (e.g., "India and China: Governance Issues and Development," *Journal of Asian Studies*, 68.2 (May 2009), 347–357), and the many references to similarities and differences between the countries that are included in Pallavi Aiyar, *Smoke and Mirrors: An Experience of China* (HarperCollins India, 2008). A wonderfully readable and carefully researched work on Xinjiang is James Millward, *Eurasian Crossroads: A History of Xinjiang* (Columbia University Press, 2007); Millward's, "The Urumqi Unrest Revisited," The China Beat, July 29, 2009, www.thechinabeat.org/?p=558, is a valuable assessment of the July 2009 unrest. See also John Gittings, "China's Uighur Conundrum," *Guardian*, July 7, 2009, www.guardian.co.uk/commentisfree/2009/jul/07/uighur-china-xinjiang-urumqi, and, for a beautifully written deeper dive into the region's past, Rian Thum, *Sacred Routes of Uyghur History* (Harvard University Press, 2014).

On gender relations in China and the Feminist Five case, see the work of Leta Hong Fincher, including *Leftover Women: The Resurgence of Gender Inequality in China*, rev. ed. (Zed Books, 2016) and "China's Feminist Five," *Dissent* (Fall 2016), https://www.dissentmagazine.org/article/china-feminist-five.

For "digital divides" and control of the Internet, see Guobin Yang, *The Power of the Internet in China: Citizen Activism Online*, 2nd ed. (Columbia University Press, 2011); Susan Shirk, ed., *Changing Media, Changing China* (Oxford, 2010); Jason Q. Ng, *Blocked on Weibo: What Gets Suppressed on China's Version of Twitter (And Why)* (The New Press, 2013); and Liz Carter, *Let 100 Voices Speak: How the Internet Is Changing China and Transforming Everyone* (I. B. Tauris, 2015). Much of the essential writing on these issues, not surprisingly, appears online, in venues such as the Berkeley-based *China Digital Times* (http://chinadigitaltimes.net/) and the Hong Kong–based China Media Project (http://cmp.hku.hk/), as well as in *Tea Leaf Nation*, available via the *Foreign Policy* website (foreignpolicy.com/channel/tea-leaf-nation/) and the Asia Society's ChinaFile online publication (http://www.chinafile.com/).

Chapter 5

For background on US–Chinese interactions and mutual images, see Jonathan Spence, *To Change China: Western Advisers in China* (Penguin, 2002); Harold R. Isaac, *Scratches on Our Minds* (M. E. Sharpe, 1980); David Arkush and Lee Ou-fan Lee, eds., *Land Without Ghosts: Chinese Impressions of America from the Mid-Nineteenth Century to the Present* (University of California Press, 1993); Scott Kennedy, ed., *China Cross-Talk* (Rowman and Littlefield, 2003); David Shambaugh, *Beautiful Imperialist: China Perceives America, 1972–1990* (Princeton University Press, 1993); Warren G. Cohen, *America's Response to China: A History of Sino-American Relations*, 5th ed. (Columbia University Press, 2010); and John Pomfret, *The Beautiful Country and the Middle Kingdom: America and China, 1776 to the Present* (Henry Holt, 2016). On the trilateral US–China–Japan relationship, see Richard McGregor, *Asia's Reckoning: China, Japan, and the Fate of U.S. Power in the Pacific Century* (Penguin Random House, 2017). Astute and accessible treatments of many issues dealt with in this chapter can be found in a trio of books edited by Lionel M. Jensen and Timothy B. Weston: *China Beyond the Headlines* (Rowman and Littlefield, 2000); *China's Transformations* (Rowman and Littlefield, 2007); and *China in and Beyond the Headlines* (Rowman and Littlefield, 2012).

On regional and other related divides, see Susan D. Blum and Lionel M. Jensen, eds., *China Off Center: Mapping the Margins of the Middle Kingdom* (University of Hawaii Press, 2002); Rob Gifford, *China Road: A Journey into the Future of a Rising Power* (Random House, 2007); and Li Cheng, "Rediscovering Urban Subcultures: The Contrast between Shanghai and Beijing," *The China Journal*, July 1996, 139–153. For ethnic variation, see Ralph Litzinger, *Other Chinas: The Yao and the Politics of National Belonging* (Duke University Press, 2000); Thomas S. Mullaney, "Introducing Critical Han Studies," *China Heritage Quarterly*, September 2009, http://www.chinaheritagequarterly.org/editorial.php?issue=019; and Sara L. Friedman, *Intimate Politics: Marriage, the Market, and State Power in Southeastern China* (Harvard University Press, 2006), which examines a group that is classified as Han but has a distinctive approach to gender relations. On generational divides, see the lively account in Duncan Hewitt, *Getting Rich First: A Modern Social History* (Pegasus, 2008); Yan Yunxiang, *Private Life Under Socialism*

(Stanford University Press, 2003) and "Little Emperors or Frail Pragmatists?" *Current History*, September 2006, 255–262; Zachary Mexico, *China Underground* (Soft Skull, 2009); Alec Ash, *Wish Lanterns: Young Lives in New China* (Picador, 2016); and Eric Fish, *China's Millennials: The Want Generation* (Rowman and Littlefield, 2015).

For further discussion of Orwell and Huxley as guides to the PRC, see Jeffrey Wasserstrom, *China's Brave New World—And Other Tales for Global Times* (Indiana University Press, 2007); and "Orwell and Huxley" in Jeffrey Wasserstrom, *Eight Juxtapositions: China through Imperfect Analogies from Mark Twain to Manchukuo* (Penguin, 2016). On the complexities of Tibet, one useful place to start is with Pico Iyer's very sympathetic but nuanced and engaging biography of its spiritual leader in exile, *The Open Road: The Global Journey of the Fourteenth Dalai Lama* (Knopf, 2008). Two insightful reviews use discussion of this book as a starting point for assessing contemporary dilemmas: Robert Barnett, "Thunder from Tibet," *New York Review of Books*, May 29, 2008, www.nybooks.com/ articles/21391; and Pankaj Mishra, "Holy Man," *New Yorker*, March 31, 2008, http://www.newyorker.com/magazine/2008/03/31/holy-man. See also the contributions to the section on Tibet in the previously cited Merkel-Hess et al., *China in 2008*.

Chapter 6

For a good introduction to the PLA, past and present, see Andrew Scobell, *China's Use of Military Force* (Cambridge University Press, 2003), and for valuable assessments of its current strength, see the chapters by Andrew S. Ericksen and Michael S. Chase in Jae Ho Chung, ed., *Assessing China's Power* (Palgrave, 2015). On Hong Kong, while there is an enormous literature on the 1997 transition, a good place to start is with John M. Carroll, *A Concise History of Hong Kong* (Rowman and Littlefield, 2007); and the admittedly idiosyncratic but lively introduction to contemporary life in the former Crown Colony provided by Leo Ou-fan Lee, *City Between Worlds: My Hong Kong* (Harvard University Press, 2008). On the Umbrella Movement, see Jason Y. Ng, *Umbrellas in Bloom: Hong Kong's Occupy Movement Uncovered* (Blacksmith Books, 2016); the Joe Piscatelli documentary, *Joshua: Teenager vs. Superpower* (2017); Sebastian Veg, "Legalistic and Utopian: Hong Kong's Umbrella Movement," *New Left Review* 92 (March–April 2015), 55–73; and Benjamin Bland, *Generation HK* (Penguin China, 2017). On Taiwan issues generally, see Nancy Bernkopf Tucker, *Strait Talk: United States-Taiwan Relations and the Crisis with China* (Harvard University Press, 2009); and Shelley Rigger, *Why Taiwan Matters: Small Island, Global Powerhouse* (Rowman and Littlefield, 2011). For the 2014 protests, see Ian Rowen, "Inside Taiwan's Sunflower Movement: Twenty-Four Days in a Student-Occupied Parliament, and the Future of the Region," *Journal of Asian Studies* 74.1 (February 2015), 5–21. Tom Miller provides a concise overview of China's shift from a country of villages to a country of cities in *China's Urban Billion: The Story Behind the Biggest Migration in Human History* (Zed Books, 2012); a sampling of academic approaches to the topic, with particular attention to comparative themes, is provided in John Logan, ed., *Urban China in Transition* (Wiley, 2008). Three compelling works of reportage that explore the human side of rural-to-urban migration are Leslie T. Chang, *Factory Girls: From Village to City in a Changing China* (Spiegel and Grau, 2007), Michelle Dammon Loyalka's elegantly crafted profiles of migrant workers, *Eating Bitterness: Stories from the Frontline of China Great Urban Migration* (University of California, 2012), and David Bandurski, *Dragons in Diamond Village: Tales of Resistance from Urbanizing China* (Penguin China, 2015).

For a far more in-depth examination of China's economy than we provide here, see Arthur Kroeber, *China's Economy: What Everyone Needs to Know* (Oxford University Press, 2016). See also, for a collection of essays on relevant themes by leading scholars of Chinese political economy, Barry Naughton and Kellee Tsai, eds., *State Capitalism, Institutional Adaptation, and the Chinese Miracle* (Cambridge University Press, 2015). On the political and economic dynamics of the One Belt, One Road Initiative (OBOR), see Alexander Cooley, "The Emerging Political Economy of OBOR: The Challenges of Promoting Connectivity in Central Asia and Beyond," Center for International and Strategic Studies, October 24, 2016, https://www.csis.org/analysis/emerging-political-economy-obor.

On China's political future and endemic problems such as corruption, some notable writings that fall at different points on the spectrum running from pessimism to optimism include Perry Link and Josh Kurlantzick, "China's Modern Authoritarianism," *Wall Street Journal*, May 25, 2009; Philip P. Pan, *Out of Mao's Shadow: The Struggle for the Soul of a New China* (Simon and Schuster, 2008); John Pomfret, *Chinese Lessons* (Holt, 2006); Ian Johnson, *Wild Grass: Three Stories of Change in Modern China* (Pantheon, 2004); Elizabeth J. Perry and Merle Goldman, eds., *Grassroots Political Reform in Contemporary China* (Harvard University Press, 2007); George J. Gilboy and Benjamin L. Read, "Political and Social Reform in China: Alive and Walking," *Washington Quarterly* (Summer

2008), 143–164; and Barmé, ed., *Red Rising, Red Eclipse*. Two recent works that emphasize the weak points and resilience of the CCP's approach to governance, respectively, are Minxin Pei, *China's Crony Capitalism: The Dynamics of Regime Decay* (Harvard University Press, 2016), and Frank Pieke, *Knowing China: A Twenty-First Century Guide* (Cambridge University Press, 2016).

On the Eighteenth Party Congress, the Bo Xilai scandal, and related 2012 events, see the "Changing of the Guard" series published by the *New York Times*, http://topics.nytimes.com/top/features/timestopics/series/changing_of_the_guard/index.html; and the coverage of this subject throughout the year in the *Economist*. See also John Garnaut, *The Rise and Fall of the House of Bo* (Penguin, 2012); for a trenchant assessment of missed opportunities during Hu's ten years in power, see Ian Johnson, "China's Lost Decade," *New York Review of Books*, September 27, 2012. On Xi Jinping, see Evan Osnos, "Born Red," *New Yorker* (April 6, 2015); Kerry Brown, *CEO China: The Rise of Xi Jinping* (I.B. Tauris, 2016); and Ian Johnson, "Xi Jinping: The Illusion of Greatness," *New York Review of Books* blog (*NYR Daily*), March 17, 2017, http://www.nybooks.com/daily/2017/03/17/xi-jinping-the-illusion-of-greatness-party-congress/.

On Chinese nationalism, good places to start in getting a sense of the range of scholarly approaches to this complex subject are Jonathan Unger, ed., *Chinese Nationalism* (M. E. Sharpe, 1996); Prasenjit Duara, *The Global and the Regional in China's Nation-Formation* (Routledge, 2009); and Henrietta Harrison, *China: Inventing the Nation* (Oxford University Press, 2001). On contemporary nationalism and its complexities, see Jessica Chen Weiss, *Powerful Patriots: Nationalist Protest in China's Foreign Relations* (Oxford University Press, 2014); Helen Gao, "Diaoyu in Our Heart: The Revealing Contradictions of Chinese Nationalism," *The Atlantic*, August 22, 2012, https://www.theatlantic.com/international/archive/2012/08/diaoyu-in-our-heart-the-revealing-contradictions-of-chinese-nationalism/261422/; and various contributions to works already mentioned, such as Rosen and Gries, *State and Society in 21st-Century China*, the Jensen and Weston volumes, Merkel-Hess et al., *China in 2008*, and Shah and Wasserstrom's *Chinese Characters*.

On energy and the environment, the best work is largely made available online through important projects such as the "China Green Project" (http://sites.asiasociety.org/chinagreen/links/), which is run through the Asia Society's Center on US–China Relations headed by Orville Schell, who has been traveling to and writing about the PRC for well over three decades; the inspiring *chinadialogue* bilingual website (www.chinadialogue.net/), which was launched by another veteran commentator on Chinese affairs, Isabel Hilton; and the Woodrow Wilson Center's "China Environment Forum" (https://www.wilsoncenter. org/program/china-environment-forum), which is run by Jennifer Turner, a specialist in PRC environmental issues. On the issue of water, see Kenneth L. Pomeranz, "The Great Himalayan Watershed," *New Left Review,* July–August 2009. See also Christina Larson's chapter in *Chinese Characters,* "Yong Yang's Odyssey."

For smart and accessible takes on a range of issues associated with Chinese environmental and economic issues, see the writing that James Fallows has done for *The Atlantic,* a sampling of which can be found in *Postcards from Tomorrow Square: Reports from China* (Vintage, 2008). See also Jonathan Watts, *When a Billion Chinese Jump* (Scribner, 2010).

The value of thinking of China and the United States as sharing a great deal is emphasized in works such as Stephen Mihm, "A Nation of Outlaws: A Century Ago, That Wasn't China—It Was Us," *Boston Globe,* August 26, 2007; various contributions to Merkel-Hess et al., *China in 2008;* Bruce Cumings, *Dominion from Sea to Sea: Pacific Ascendancy and American Power* (Yale University Press, 2009); and Evan Osnos, *Age of Ambition: Chasing Fortune, Truth, and Faith in the New China* (FSG, 2014). See also Howard W. French, "Letter from China: China Could Use Some Honest Talk about Race," *International Herald Tribune,* July 31, 2009, http://www.nytimes.com/2009/08/01/world/asia/01iht-letter.html, which usefully places side by side the riots that erupted in Detroit in July 1967 and those that took place in Xinjiang in July 2009.

For a frequently revised and updated list of our favorite online resources, including China-focused websites, podcasts, Twitter feeds, and more, please see bit.ly/MoreChina.

INDEX